E. Lynn "Fox

Ferrets

Everything About
Housing, Care, Nutrition, Breeding,
and Health Care

Filled with Full-color Photographs
Illustrations by Michele Earle-Bridges

BARRON'S

2 CONTENTS

IS A FERRET RIGHT FOR YOU?

Introduction

I encountered my first ferret in a pet store in 1978. The charming little fur ball fascinated me, but I was reluctant to take him home because I knew nothing about ferret care, their body language or temperament. Was it a wild animal? Did it bite? What should I feed this baby? Would it play? Did it like other animals? I had five dogs at that time. Could it be litter trained? And most important—would it love me back? Unfortunately, the store clerk knew only that it was sweet, docile, and playful. My caution prevailed and I left without the slinky, furry creature.

After extensive research in books, pet stores, and visits with several small breeders, the first ten ferrets came to what was to become Path Valley Farm—and completely captured my heart. A sable female I named Crystal was to become a constant companion. Crystal loved to ride in coat hoods, begged for red licorice treats and became goodwill ambassador for ferrets during her visits to the local library book programs. Sleeping peacefully in my lap, shuffling along under my feet and playing with wild abandon—she was everything you could ask for in a companion. It hardly seemed possible to pack so much personality into such a small body.

It's easy to fall instantly in love with a ferret, but it's important to do the research before deciding to keep one as a pet.

Eventually a breeding colony of 75 ferrets came to live at Path Valley Farm. Males, when available, of suitable temperament, conformation, and markings were added. Mothers needed to be productive, but that was just the beginning. Docile temperament, wide catlike heads, and good markings are of great importance. Early on, Path Valley Farm aimed at producing ferrets likely to live as long and healthy a life as possible. This has always been a priority in our breeding program. We feel our breeding program helps give PVF ferrets somewhat of a genetic edge in this area.

Path Valley Farm does not sell ferrets for research or fur. PVF is a "pets only" farm. Although the ferret colony has grown quite large over the years, the babies are all loved, handled, tickled, kissed, and played with by all of us here at PVF before they can leave for new homes. This will continue to be our policy.

Ferrets are still misunderstood, but things are much better now than in 1978 when I first searched for information.

Most people are now familiar with the fact that ferrets are a domestic animal just like cats and dogs.

It is common knowledge that the female ferret really can die if left in heat during the entire breeding season. She must be spayed or kept continually bred.

Nearly all ferrets are now neutered and de-scented before being sold. This is done to protect the ferret from health risks.

There are textbooks for veterinarians to learn about ferrets—there were none in the early years.

There is an approved rabies vaccine for ferrets.

There are many excellent products on the market just for ferrets. These include ferret feed, cages, shampoos, toys and many other wonderful and safe products.

Before You Buy

Adding a new family member is an important decision—one that should never be made on impulse no matter how adorable the soft furry kits (babies) are. You must be prepared to make a time commitment to any new animal. In all fairness to the ferret, stop and consider these points:

✔ A ferret will require care. You must make sure he or she has fresh food and water. The cage must be cleaned and the litter changed as needed. Can you do this?

✔ Are you prepared to spend the time required getting acquainted with the new baby? If this is a very busy time in your life, would postponing the decision be better?

✔ If you rent your apartment or house, have you checked to be sure you will be allowed to keep a ferret?

✔ What will you do when vacation time comes? Is there room in the car for a cage, or is there someone who can care for your ferret while you are away?

✔ Have you checked local and state laws to ensure ferrets are not forbidden in your area? (See page 89.)

✔ Ferrets require neutering (spaying in females and castration in males) to be good, healthy pets. Female ferrets often die from aplastic anemia if they are not neutered. Male ferrets can become overly aggressive if not neutered. Ferrets sold by reputable stores and breeders usually will have already had this surgery performed to protect them. Can you obtain neutered ferrets somewhere near you, or are you prepared for the surgical expense of an unaltered ferret?

✔ Ferrets should be de-scented—preferably *before* you purchase your pet—to reduce their odor and to eliminate any future risk of infected or blocked scent glands (see page 63). The majority of ferrets sold today will have already had this operation completed. If you are not able to find a ferret that was de-scented before purchase, can you find a veterinarian who routinely does this surgery? Are you willing to incur this expense?

✔ Ferrets, like all pets, require regular veterinary care both for routine physicals and vaccinations and care for treatable diseases as your pet ages. Are you prepared for this expense?

✔ If the ferret is to belong to your child, is he or she really willing to love and care for the pet every day for years to come?

✔ Ferrets require one of the special ferret foods now on the market. Ferret food formulated to meet the high animal protein and high fat needs of your ferret is readily available at pet stores today. Good feed is less expensive than the veterinarian bills which can result from poor nutrition. A kit fed a poor-quality diet will be nippy and likely to have health problems later in life if the diet is not improved.

✔ Kits can be overzealous in their play and nip too hard. Will you be able to, when necessary,

Training your ferret will probably involve a fair amount of scolding and consistent discipline.

scold and discipline your kit? Consistent discipline is part of loving the animal in a responsible manner.

✔ With good care, the ferret will live for 7 or more years. Are you prepared for a long-term commitment?

✔ Babies or young children should not be left unsupervised with any pets. This includes ferrets. This is for the safety of both the ferret and the child. The child could accidentally harm such a small pet. The ferret, even though tiny, has sharp teeth like a puppy or kitten and should be supervised by an adult.

✔ Do you have other pets in the rodent family? If so, you must keep in mind that ferrets are mousers. The other pets must be kept in a safe environment.

Clockwise from top left, a Blaze, a Sable, and a Cinnamon enjoying the couch.

This Red-eyed White is sleeping blissfully.

A Blaze face can occur in a variety of color choices.

A Blaze curls up after abandoning his favorite toy.

10 TIPS

For New Ferret Owners
(From *Modern Ferret* magazine)

1 Find a good veterinarian.
A good ferret veterinarian is important for helping your pet lead a long and healthy life. Ferrets require annual vaccinations against rabies and distemper. A new kit should always visit a veterinarian immediately for a check-up, and at that time you can discuss a vaccination schedule. Also, he or she can show you methods for proper ear cleaning, nail clipping, and dental hygiene techniques.

2 Stock up on food and treats.
Today, there are many high-quality ferret foods on the market. Remember, a healthy balanced diet is of utmost importance to your ferret's health and longevity. Ferrets are carnivores, so be sure to include meat as one of their staple ingredients. It's a good idea to introduce the ferret to multiple brands of food. Be sure to offer food and water at all times. Kits will need their food moistened for them until their teeth and jaws are developed and ready for hard food. Remember, multiple treats are not a substitute for good food.

3 Litter box training.
With some effort on your part, ferrets can be trained to use a litter box (see Appendix 2, page 90). Ferrets naturally like to go in the spot where they went before, and they seem to prefer backing into cor-

ners. They will always avoid evacuating in places where they eat, sleep, and play. It's important that you encourage proper litter box usage by (1) providing enough litter boxes in the cage and the rooms they play in (ferrets don't like to travel far once they decide they need to use the litter box) and (2) discourage them from going in the wrong places by putting down food bowls, blankets, or toys.

4 Grooming.
Ferrets are generally clean creatures, but they will require some grooming help, including regular ear cleaning and nail clipping. Ferret-specific ear cleaning solutions are available in pet stores, and nail clipping is best done while the ferret is distracted (rub a treat on his belly and trim his nails while he licks it off!) Ferrets should be bathed when they get dirty, but be sure not to bathe them too often—this will only prompt them to release more of their natural oils, which can make them smell muskier. When your ferret is shedding, administer a hairball remedy to help him pass any fur he swallows.

5 Odor control.
Ferrets have a natural musky smell that will always be around, but there are other scents you'll probably want to reduce. Keep litter boxes clean, and clean

the bedding regularly—that should reduce most unpleasant odors. Ferrets that are not spayed or neutered will have a very strong smell, so try to get one that has already been treated (see page 16).

6 Nip training and socializing.
Ferrets are social animals, and they love to play. They are smart, and will play properly, but only *if you expect it of them*. They play with other ferrets by mock combat—it is your responsibility to teach them that play with humans is not like that. They will learn if you teach them. A mother ferret disciplines her kits by the scruff of the neck—you can do the same. Don't hit your ferret, but work gently with him to let him know what you expect. Offer lickable treats from your hands, and give the ferret some of his own toys to play with. Work with the ferret's natural desires to run around and play, and curl up and snuggle.

7 Housing.
For their protection, ferrets should be caged when you are not around to supervise. Curiosity will get them into dangerous situations they may not be able to escape. Your ferret's cage should be a safe haven where he feels comfortable, with food, water, a litter box, and sleeping blankets or hammocks. They should be housed in a wire cage with soft covering over the entire floor so as to protect their paws.

8 Ferret proofing.
Ferrets are extremely curious and intelligent, and that can sometimes mean problems for you and your home. They will always try to climb things, get into things, out of things and under things. Ferret proofing is an ongoing process of getting down to their level and ensuring there is nothing harmful or dangerous they can get into. Beware also of toys with small, plastic parts that can be chewed off and swallowed—this can lead to serious digestive tract blockage.

9 Play and intellectual stimulation.
Ferrets require exercise and intellectual stimulation on a daily basis. "Toys" as simple as an empty box or a dangling towel will give them much enjoyment. By providing your pet with intellectual stimulation, you'll also be preventing possible destructive behavior that comes from stress and boredom. The amount of play a ferret requires depends on his age and health, but young ferrets require several hours a day.

10 Respect.
Ferrets are living creatures, and you need to consider it seriously before adopting one. Like children, they need to be taught right from wrong, they will make mistakes, and they need affection and attention. If you care for them and appreciate both their good points and their faults, they will be loving and amusing companions unlike any other animal.

ACQUIRING YOUR FERRET

Once you have decided that a ferret is right for you, you should make a few preliminary decisions before you purchase a pet. Do you want a male or a female? One ferret or two? Do you want a baby kit or an adult? You must also be sure that you purchase a healthy animal from a reputable dealer.

Male or Female?

Choosing the color and sex of your new ferret is strictly a matter of personal preference. Males and females require about the same amount of space and time. Both are equally hardy. The sexes do not differ greatly in behavior; ferrets have individual personalities. Neither sex nor a particular color will influence the nature of the pet.

Male and female kits start out at about the same size. However, the mature male is about twice the size of the mature female. Males will range from 3 to 5 pounds (1.5–2.5 kg), while females grow to a mere 1½ to 3 pounds (0.75–1.5 kg).

Neutered and de-scented ferrets have very little odor, but a spayed and de-scented female has the least odor of all. After all, with females, you have only half as many pounds of ferret in the house as you would with males.

Females must be spayed unless repeatedly bred at each heat. Otherwise, they frequently

The Sable ferret is the most commonly bred, but there are many color options to choose from.

develop a serious disease called aplastic anemia and die. The cost of spaying should be considered before acquiring a female. (Obviously, the cost of neutering a male ferret must also be considered if you are unable to obtain one that has been altered and de-scented.)

My tip: As previously mentioned, the majority of the animals sold today will have been de-scented and neutered. However, asking the breeder or pet store dealer about both operations before completing your purchase is wise.

Which Color?

A number of colors are now being bred: sable (the most common color), red-eyed white, silver-mitt, sterling silver, white-footed sable, butterscotch, white-footed butterscotch, and the beautiful cinnamon ferret.

Many unusual variations are now available. We regularly see black-eyed whites with a stripe down the back, spotted babies, blazes on the face, pale silvers with dark markings on one leg or the tail, color rings on the tail, and color shade variations of every variety. While we attempt to describe some color basics, too many colors are available to cover them all. Temperament and longevity are the cornerstones of our breeding program here at Path Valley Farm, and color variations have been prized and enhanced from the very beginning in 1978.

Sable: With marks and masks like raccoons, understanding their popularity is easy. Sables range widely from light to dark, depending on the shade of both the underfur and guard hairs. The underfur ranges from white to beige. This fur will sometimes have a slight golden cast to it. The guard hairs are longer and are black. A well-marked sable ferret should have a definite mask or hood pattern over the face. The preferred nose color is black to match the trim. The face should be short and broad.

Red-Eyed White: This color is frequently referred to as albino. Red-eyed whites range in color from white to golden; some are albinos and some are not. Only through breeding can this be determined. Noses are, of course, pink. Especially important in the whites is for the animal to have a short, broad head. A ferret should in no way resemble a rat.

Silver-Mitt: The underfur of the silver-mitt is white or off-white. The guard hair contains both black and white strands. This mix is what accounts for the silvery appearance. A silver-mitt ferret will also have four white feet and a white bib. The eyes appear black or a deep burgundy.

Sterling Silver: The sterling-silver ferret is marked like the silver-mitt. The difference is in the ratio of black to white guard hairs. The sterling silver has considerably more white strands in the guard hair, thus giving it a much paler appearance than the regular medium-silver shade.

White-Footed Sable: This ferret is marked like a standard sable ferret but has four white feet and a white throat patch. Not all show the throat patch characteristic. The white-footed sable does not have white guard hairs as does the silver. Noses are generally black.

Butterscotch: The underfur of the butterscotch ferret is the same as that of the sable. However, the guard hairs, leggings, and mask

or hood patterns are butterscotch rather than black. Noses are generally butterscotch to match the guards.

White-Footed Butterscotch: Although marked like a butterscotch, this ferret has the four white feet and white throat patch of the silver-mitts.

Cinnamon: Truly beautiful! The underfur is white or off-white. The guard hair is the rich red-brown color of cinnamon.

Black-Eyed Whites: The black-eyed white ferret has a white body but black eyes. You may still find a few black guard hairs on the back or tail. The animal should give the appearance of having a white body.

Stripes: This ferret will give the bold appearance of having a stripe down the back. The stripe may be black, butterscotch, or cinnamon in color.

Spotted: Spotting appears on the stomach or can cover the back. Spotted kits often have possum-looking marking on their faces. We now see spotted adults with white bodies and a striking splash of black at the back of one leg.

In addition to the above colors, Path Valley Farm has been breeding ferrets of colors too rare to have their own category as of yet. These include such varieties as the white-foot sable with a white head, silvers with one dark side and one light side, light colors with dark vests, and so on. There are some truly rare, beautiful color varieties developing as of press time.

What Age?

A well-cared-for ferret generally lives for 7 or more years. When selecting a pet, remember that both kits and adults have advantages and disadvantages.

A kit can be a great source of joy to raise and train. If you are new to ferrets, kits are less intimidating because they are so tiny. On the other hand, kits require more time to train. They need consistent discipline for housebreaking and for avoiding too-rough play. They can also be rowdy adolescents before becoming settled adults.

Adult ferrets—if they have been well handled—are past all these stages. However, adults who have not been handled with love and discipline are poor choices and are best left to experts. A grown ferret has the ability to adapt to and love the new family quickly. After only a short time, you will be amazed at how easily the adult becomes a member of the family. Perhaps it will already be litter or cage trained. If not, it can still learn and be disciplined. Another advantage with an adult is that you can see the animal's exact size, coat color, and marking pattern. As with the kit, purchasing an adult that has already been neutered and de scented is less expensive. If the adult has not been altered, be sure to check with your veterinarian regarding the cost of surgery before purchasing your ferret.

The final decision comes down to which ferret you find and fall in love with. If it is a kit, you will have a great learning experience together. If it is an adult, the ferret will quickly learn to love you as if you had raised him or her yourself.

One Ferret, a Pair, or a Group?

Ferrets are social animals. One ferret, when given some playtime and toys, will entertain itself and you quite successfully. If possible, place the animal's housing near an activity-oriented section of your home such as the kitchen, living room, or dining area. Because ferrets are so active, they sleep up to 14 hours per day. If they have nothing interesting to do, ferrets tend to catch some shut-eye; thus, the ferret is ready to play and explore when you have the time. Ferrets are frequently caged for their own safety at night or while everyone is away. You should allow your ferret some freedom to explore and play out of the cage under supervision during at least part of your time at home. If you already have a dog or cat, the ferret will soon teach that pet some new tricks and games.

If you are contemplating buying a pair of ferrets, you should know that they need not be purchased together. Most adult ferrets will—after a very short adjustment period—accept another adult or a kit. If you have very little time for your pets, a pair of ferrets will keep each other company. They will, however, still want some freedom and a chance to include you in their games. The fun of watching two ferrets roll and tumble together more than compensates for the additional work. They prefer to live in the same cage and can use the same bowls.

A word of caution: Unneutered males should not be housed with other ferrets. They become so territorial during breeding season that serious injury or death for the other ferret can result.

Groups of ferrets are as much fun as a circus. We know a young couple who has converted their spare bedroom into a ferret playground. It contains slides and sandboxes, and tubes made from a 4-inch (10 cm) plastic drainage pipe that make up a giant tunnel system. An old handbag

Neutered ferrets make for better pets all the way around.

suspended on a rope and spring created a swing that bounces up and down. There are crinkly bags for the ferrets to jump on and crawl into and out of. The ferrets even have a remote-control car to chase and capture. This couple says, "It's more fun to have friends over to watch the ferrets than to go to the movies." Many wonderful ferret toys and tubes are now on the market to provide a stimulating environment for your ferret.

Neutered, De-Scented, or Both?

Neutered and de-scented ferret kits are available nearly anywhere in this country now; and they are by far your best choice. If you are unable to find a neutered and de-scented ferret, you will want to have this surgery done as early as possible. Be sure to check with your veterinarian concerning the cost of these

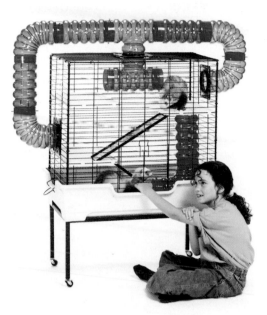

Welcome to ferret playland! Ferrets love to run through tubes such as these shown here.

as a cuddly pet—but it takes more than 30 days for musk secretions to stop. Moreover, the aggression level of unneutered males becomes high enough to require them to be housed separately.

Female ferrets, under natural lighting conditions and kept outside, come into heat about February and remain in heat through September (they do *not* cycle in and out of heat during this period like most mammals). This prolonged heat cycle and its concurrent high levels of estrogen lead to aplastic anemia and septicemia. This condition can cause about 90 percent of all females left unbred to die during their first spring-summer after birth. Unless the female is to be kept as a breeder, *she must be spayed.* De-scenting at this time is a good idea

surgeries before you purchase a ferret that is not already neutered and de-scented.

If you purchase an unneutered male ferret, your baby will begin to smell and secrete so much musk he will become greasy to the touch during breeding season. Unless you plan on keeping him and starting a serious breeding farm, you will want to attend to this early on and avoid this unpleasant situation.

Even a grown, smelly male can be neutered and de-scented and will regain his desirability

The litter box should be low in front for easy access.

for odor control and to eliminate any possible health risks from infected scent glands. Many veterinarians prefer to perform this de-scenting surgery at the same time they spay or castrate a ferret.

Ferrets have anal scent glands. Like skunks, which have a special adaptation enabling them to use their glands as an offensive weapon, ferrets can expel an unpleasant odor. However, they do so only in fear of their life, for example, during rough handling or if playing with other ferrets gets out of hand. This ferret spray, however, is not to be confused with skunk spray. Ferret spray dispels in an average room within minutes and washes off easily with soap and water.

If your ferret has not been de-scented by the time you take him home, the procedure should definitely be done, since plugged scent glands can be a recurrent problem. Evidence indicates that de-scenting does lower the odor level of both males and females.

My tip: Purchasing a ferret that is already neutered and de-scented is safest. Then, your pet will not face these risks.

Where to Purchase a Ferret

No matter where you purchase your pet, the most important element is the knowledge of the seller. In your first experience with an unfamiliar animal, you will have many questions. An experienced seller can allay unfounded fears and help handle any real problems you may encounter—from health to training to tricks. The two most common sources of pet ferrets are pet stores and small, local breeders.

From a Pet Store

Most areas have an abundance of pet stores. You can find them through ads in your phone book and newspapers and from recommendations by friends.

A well-recommended pet shop should be your first choice for shopping for a ferret. It's a good idea to visit as many stores as you can and compare quality carefully. A low price can never make up for a poor-quality ferret with health or behavioral problems. You should be able to obtain a ferret that is already neutered and de-scented. The ferret should be both playful and docile in temperament.

A clean, well-lighted, and well-run pet store is a real treat for all animal lovers. The excitement of seeing all the animals, plus a wide selection of items for your pet, makes for a worthwhile visit.

Unfortunately, some stores do not meet these expectations. A few owners allow their stores to become a motley collection of ill-kept animals. However, the majority of pet stores do provide the best possible animals and supplies.

Here is what to look for in a good pet shop:
✔ All animals should appear healthy, be active when appropriate, and be in suitable enclosures.
✔ All areas and enclosures should be clean and odor-free.
✔ Feeding and watering equipment should be clean and algae-free.
✔ A wide selection of food, simple medicines, toys, cages, and training equipment for each species should be available.
✔ Lighting should be suitable for each species.
✔ The staff should be clean and well-groomed.
✔ A selection of books about animals should be available.

✔ The pet shop owner and the employees should be willing to gather information and make it available to you.

✔ Both the name of who bred your ferret and a written guarantee should be available to you. Some ferret breeders raise pets only and will not raise ferrets for research or fur. If this is an issue for you, be sure to check before you buy your ferret. The name of the breeder plus whether he or she is a pets-only breeder will be on the written guarantee. Be sure to read and compare guarantees to see just what is covered. Some may guarantee only that the ferret is neutered and de-scented while others guarantee against any potential genetic defects for some specific amount of time.

✔ The shop should have a good reputation with other customers and with local business groups. A phone call to these references is time well spent before making a major purchase. The pet store should be willing to provide the name and telephone number of a veterinarian you can call for a reference.

Remember that, because of the order of jobs to be done, not all these factors are possible at every moment of the day. After all, some cages must be cleaned first and some last. However, over the course of several visits, you should not see any single area neglected. Such neglect is a good reason to avoid the store.

From a Local Breeder

Local breeders can be found through their ads in newspapers in the column about pets and in small direct ad papers. When visiting a small breeder, remember the following dos and do nots.

✔ **Do** call ahead for an appointment. This saves wasted trips and ensures you that the breeder will have the time available to help you select a pet and provide you with the information you need.

✔ **Do** ask to see the parents of the kits. The personality, size, and temperament of the parents are reflected in their offspring.

✔ **Do** ask to see a selection, if possible. A group of playing ferrets will tell you about the behavior of the individual kits.

✔ **Do** ask if the ferret has already been neutered and de-scented. If not, ask about veterinarians in the area who do these operations, and check about the cost.

✔ **Do** observe the general condition of the facility. A clean, well-kept breeding area indicates that the breeder cares for the animals and that your kit will be well on its way toward good health.

✔ **Do** compare the breeder's written guarantee with the one from the pet store.

✔ **Do** ask the breeder to provide a reference from a veterinarian.

✔ **Do** ask lots of questions. How long has the breeder been breeding ferrets? How many animals does he or she have? What are the names and phone numbers of other customers?

✔ **Do not** take other animals along. Other pets may bring fleas, colds, and disease germs to the breeding colony.

✔ **Do not** take people with colds or other infectious illnesses with you.

✔ **Do not** let children under six years of age play with animals they do not know.

✔ **Do not** buy on impulse, no matter how cute the kits are.

An active, intelligent animal who lives for 7 or more years should be a well-thought-out purchase. Any reputable breeder should have knowledge and in-depth experience with ferrets of all ages and offer personal service and advice

Left: Cages provide safety for your ferrets when you are not home to supervise their antics.
Below: A good example of a ferret cage, but be wary of letting a new kit on the ramps— it's apt to take a tumble and get an injury.

about keeping ferrets. Unfortunately, many breeders do not meet these high standards. Do check carefully before choosing a breeder.

Signs of a Healthy Ferret

In selecting your ferret, you should look for the following:

1. Bright, clear eyes of even size. Some ferrets suffer from very small eyes (microphthalmia). Secretions of any kind indicate infection or irritation.

2. No nasal discharge, clean ears, and good teeth.

3. Long, full whiskers. Short, broken whiskers indicate poor nutrition and sometimes infections.

4. No large lumps on the body. These lumps may be cancerous.

5. A soft, full coat. The guard or long hairs should be firm enough to stand out from the soft wool of the undercoat.

6. Firm and even distribution of muscle. The ferret should appear long, muscular, and athletic as an adult. Healthy kits have large, full bellies.

7. Clean genital areas. Feces around the anal area indicate diarrhea,

and secretions around the vulva or penis are signs of genitourinary infections.

8. Good temperament and attitude. The prospective pet should be playful and gentle. Play biting and mock combat are a normal occurrence. Painful bites or overly aggressive attitudes should be avoided.

9. Curiosity. A socialized kit should have no fear of new people, objects, or sounds. A confident attitude is the mark of a healthy and happy ferret.

Expenses of Purchase and Maintenance

Prices vary, but remember to check both the quality of the baby and the guarantee. Sometimes prices vary because you are comparing different-quality ferrets. The goal should be to choose the best pet—one who will live a long healthy life as a part of your family. The more unusual colors sometimes cost somewhat more. (If you are considering an animal that is not yet neutered and de-scented, check on the cost of these surgeries in your area.) The purchase price is much less than that for other animals of similar intelligence and life span such as purebred dogs, cats, and birds. The cage, toys, and supplies of high-quality ferret food and other equipment varies widely. Of course, buying a cage of almost any price is possible.

A single adult ferret will consume as much as 5 to 8 pounds (2.5–4 kg) of high-quality dry ferret food per month. Premium quality

A harness is one of the first purchases you'll need to make when you buy a new ferret.

Furniture Protection

Speaking of expenses that come along with a new ferret, there is always the possibility (or probability!) that furniture repair may be necessary before your new pet is fully house-trained. Following is a brief list of suggestions for keeping furniture damage to a minimum in the first stages of ferret ownership:

Rugs: Many ferrets dig at the carpet, especially near closed doors. Until your ferret is trained that this is a no-no, you should consider covering sections of your rug that the ferret prefers with a plastic carpet protector. Once he realizes he's not getting the "shred-ability factor" he desires, he's likely to give up. Carpet protectors are readily available in office supply stores.

Cabinets: Forever curious and eager to explore, ferrets will always try squeezing into your kitchen and bathroom cabinets.

Depending on the design, most cabinets will deny access to a ferret using just a strong tape or rubber bands around two handles. However, extremely inquisitive ferrets will only be deterred by child-proof locks and latch-and-key systems. Try your local hardware store for the best advice.

Beds: The inside of box springs are favorite hiding places for ferrets. They often rip the cloth on the bottom and climb inside. This can obviously be dangerous, so try attaching a fitted sheet to the bottom of the box spring, secured with tacks or small nails.

Plants: Houseplants are fair game for a ferret's digging and chewing instincts, so be certain not to bring any poisonous plants into your home. You can prevent digging by covering the soil with rocks or a metal mesh over the pot.

ferret food is usually slightly more expensive than cat food, but the ferret will tend to consume less because this food is more concentrated. Feed consumption varies with your ferret's coat changes. Ferrets have a heavier, thicker coat for part of the year and a thinner coat at other times of the year. Before your ferret gets this thicker coat, he or she will consume more food and increase in weight. After the heavier coat is fully grown, the ferret will

generally consume less food and repeat the cycle. Thus, food is not a major cost item for the maintenance of ferrets.

Ferrets can be easily groomed at home. The cost of professional grooming should not be an issue.

A yearly visit to the veterinarian is essential for distemper shots, rabies shots, if indicated, and a general health checkup. Costs vary widely for this service, so check in advance.

ACQUIRING THE FERRET'S PET SUPPLIES

Once you have decided that you wish to keep a ferret or several ferrets, you must prepare appropriate housing. You must obtain the equipment you will need to care for the animals and make them healthy and happy.

Housing

Your ferret's house can be a multilevel condo, a cage, or a small room in the house that has been ferret proofed. You can even let your ferret live outside year round. However, if you want to do this, be sure to place the ferret outside for the first time during the summer. Then he or she will be able to adjust gradually to changes in temperature and cooler weather as winter approaches. If the ferret is left outside, the animal should have some shade—ferrets cannot tolerate high temperatures and should not be in direct sunlight. Your pet will also need a small box or soft cloth to curl up in for sleeping. In the winter, you must provide straw or other warm nesting material. A roof should be over the whole cage to protect the ferret from wind and weather. Temperatures greater than 90°F (32°C) can be life threatening to your ferret. Depending on the specific

Let's play! Ferrets love to crawl in and out of holes.

conditions, temperatures over 80°F (27°C) can even produce heatstroke in your pet.

Another added risk besides weather is heartworms. While ferrets cannot transmit heartworms, they can get them from the bite of an infected mosquito. This is especially a concern in the southern part of the United States if your ferret is routinely outside. Be sure to consult your veterinarian as this disease can be prevented.

If you decide to house your ferret in a cage—and most people do—you can find many cages or ferret condos through your pet store, on the internet, or through suppliers advertising in ferret magazines. No matter how large or deluxe the ferret housing becomes, your ferret should also have substantial time out of the cage for play and socialization activities each day. Any cage design should provide a litter area, a feeding area, and a sleeping area. Ferrets like to get into a dark and private area to really relax and sleep. Each cage should be equipped with a box, fabric bag, or tube where the ferret can go to get away and curl up in the dark. This is a natural part of what a ferret needs in a busy household.

The deluxe ferret condos may have several levels, hanging hammocks, tubes in which the ferret loves to play, plus eating and litter pan areas. Note that when you first bring your baby home, the baby should not be allowed to climb to the upper levels. A small baby could climb high enough to step off, fall, and become injured. Just pull up the ramps to the upper levels until the baby has grown a little larger.

Aquariums are not recommended for ferret cages because they allow for poor air circulation. Either choosing a cage specifically designed for ferrets or completely ferret proofing one small room in the house (see Hidden Home Dangers, page 59) is best. Remember, if the ferret can get his or her head through an opening, the ferret can squeeze his or her body out of the opening.

The Litter Box

The ferret's litter box should have a low edge in the front and three high sides. The one low edge allows the ferret to climb in and out of the box more easily. Since ferrets back all the way into a corner to urinate or defecate, you will want three high sides to prevent accidents over the edge. Leaving some feces in the litter

box until your ferret is completely trained is a good idea. This helps to discourage the animal from playing in the litter. Any litter suitable for cats is fine for ferrets.

For a very basic idea of how to litter train a new ferret, refer to Appendix 2 on page 91.

The Sleeping Area

The ferret needs a special nesting spot with appropriate bedding material for sleeping. The choice of nesting spot and bedding depends on the type of cage you use. If you are using a wire cage, the ferret will be happier with a small box for a hidey-hole. Your ferret will enjoy crawling in and out of the box and will not be happy with just a bare wire cage with no enclosed hiding spot. An upright tissue box or a plastic milk jug with holes cut out in several places makes a good ferret bedroom. The nest house should be affixed to one end of the cage so it will not end up being moved to the litter end of the cage and becoming soiled.

If the cage and attached nesting box are to be kept outdoors, the bedding material can be any soft, insulating material. You should avoid cedar chips, which have been known to cause respiratory problems in ferrets, and also sawdust, which can cause eye irritation. Pine chips should also be avoided for ferrets. Aspen chips are available at most pet stores and are safe for ferrets.

If the cage and attached nesting box are to be kept indoors, the nesting material can be soft cloth, cotton preferably. A soft cotton T-shirt, old towel, or imitation sheepskin makes

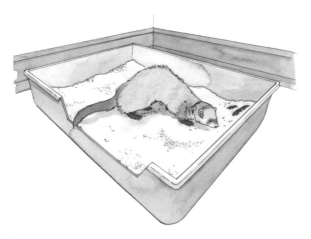

Leaving some feces in the litter until your ferret is fully trained is a good idea.

a nice sleeping cover and can be washed easily. Loose strings are a danger to your ferret because they can be swallowed and form an intestinal blockage. If you see loose strings, remove the material immediately and replace it. There are a variety of ferret beddings available at most pet stores today.

If you use a cage with a closed bottom, one section of it should be provided with bedding materials to serve as a sleeping corner. Any of the nesting materials mentioned above would be appropriate. The ferret will still need a dark sleeping box to hide out.

Food and Water Dishes

All ferrets need a constant supply of fresh food and water. You should purchase the food dishes and water bottles carefully and clean them daily.

A heavy earthenware dish or shallow bowl is best for dry food. A lightweight dish is easily dumped and converted to a toy. Ferrets are strong for their body size and love to play with their dishes. If a lightweight dish is used, it must be attached to the cage so the ferret cannot move it. Be sure to place the food into the sleeping area of the cage, not near the litter area where it can become soiled.

Water should also be supplied in the sleeping area. As I said, ferrets need a constant supply of fresh water, and one easy way to supply this is to use water bottles that can be affixed to the side of the cage. Be sure, however, to attach the bottles low enough for the ferret to reach the spout easily. With a new kit, touch his or her nose to the spout so that the animal knows where the water is. A heavy crock bowl with fresh water should be available until you

Ferrets will easily tip water bowls, so remember, the heavier the better.

see your ferret using the water bottle regularly. If the ferret does not know how to use the water bottle, he or she can easily become dehydrated. This could be a life-threatening situation even though water is available. Be absolutely sure your ferret uses the water bottle on a regular basis before removing the water bowl from the cage.

Grooming Aids

You need certain items to keep your ferret well-groomed. Purchasing these items as soon as you bring your ferret home is best. In that way, you will always be prepared to give your pet a bath and proper grooming. Remember, though, too-frequent bathing can strip essential oils and lead to itchy skin. Once a month is usually enough.

You need the following:
✔ tearless shampoo approved for ferrets or cats—for bathing,
✔ a regular bathroom towel—for drying,

Ferrets need a constant supply of fresh water, so water bottles attached to the cage are a good idea.

A sampling of ferret supplies. It's important to note that a harness should be left on only when the ferret is supervised and on a leash—when in the house or a cage, a breakaway collar is sufficient.

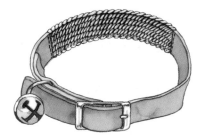

✔ ordinary fingernail clippers—for trimming nails,
✔ an ordinary nail file—for filing nails, and
✔ a stiff brush—to remove hair during the twice-yearly coat changes.

Collars and Harnesses

Keeping a collar on your ferret is wise. If your pet should escape, the collar instantly alerts someone unfamiliar with ferrets that this is a pet. It is *not* some strange wild animal.

The ferret collar should be soft and lightweight. Nylon, suede, or soft leather is fine. If the collar is too bulky, the ferret will remove it. A small bell can be attached to the collar. This makes locating your pet in the house easier.

Ferrets can be trained to walk in harnesses. For walking, use an escape-proof harness for safety and then remove it when your walk is finished. For wearing every day, the ferret should have a collar with an elastic insert that will enable the ferret to escape should he or she become stuck or trapped in an emergency situation. Ferret harnesses are readily available in pet stores.

Toys

Any item that appeals to the ferret's sense of curiosity and adventure will be a treat for your

A small bell on your ferret's collar makes him easier to find in the house.

pet. A good example of this is a clean plastic gallon jug with several 3-inch (7.5 cm) holes. The jug thus transformed may become a sleeping area, but can also become a playhouse, jungle trail, secret hideout, and perfect obstacle course for a game of chase.

Today, there are many safe ferret toys available on the market. Ferrets do not find catnip appealing but do accept toys containing it. Be especially vigilant with any small item that the ferret could swallow and that could get lodged in the intestines. This is a life-threatening situation requiring surgery for your pet. Rubber toys are particularly dangerous to ferrets as small chunks of rubber can break off and be swallowed. Veterinarians have reported removing chunks of rubber toys, chunks of tennis shoe soles, chunks of soap, squeaky-toy squeakers, peanuts, Legos, doll shoes, and many other small items the ferret may play with and swallow.

Plastic pipe 3 inches (7.5 cm) in diameter and with angles provides your ferret with a safe place to explore. The more turns and corners in the pipe, the better.

Hammocks, carry pouches, and tunnels are also fun supplies available for your ferret.

Training Aids

You can use several products to help you when you try to train your ferret. The vitamin-rich liquid Ferretone is a treat for ferrets—they love it. It can be used as a reward for your ferret when he or she does what you wish, or it can be used to reinforce good experiences.

Give a kit a drop or two when you pick up the kit and he or she will associate being picked up with a treat.

Ferretone is an excellent coat supplement as well, helping to keep the fur smooth and furry. Be careful not to use too much, however. Limit the Ferretone treats to two to three drops a day. The daily recommended dosage of Ferretone is ¾ teaspoon (3.75 mL) per day for adult ferrets and 1½ teaspoons (7.5 mL) per day for kits, or pregnant and nursing females. Be sure to consult the bottle for updated measurements. A hair-coloring applicator bottle or similar type of squeeze bottle is a handy way to dispense the treat. Any treat your ferret likes will work as a training aid. Many ferrets like raisins (please be sure to cut them up first), cooked meat, fruit, or vegetables. Be sure to remember these are just treats and should be given in tiny amounts. They should never replace a balanced diet or your ferret may become ill.

Just as ferrets like Ferretone and will associate happy experiences with it, they dislike Bitter Apple. It can be used to train a ferret not to touch something. For example, ferrets sometimes become fascinated with curly telephone cords. Bitter Apple can be sprayed on the cord several times a day. After a few days, the ferret will lose all interest in chewing on the cord.

Do not forget perhaps the two best training aids—your voice and your hands. Talk to your ferret. When he or she behaves well, speak in a soothing manner. If your ferret acts badly, a sharp "No" or "Stop" is quite effective. A ferret should be treated much like a new puppy.

CHECKLIST

Disciplining Your Ferret

Not all ferrets respond well to nose-flicking, especially if your pet was mistreated or abused before you brought him home. Here are a few alternative ideas for letting your pet know he needs to calm down.

✔ Try yelling "Hey!" in as deep a commanding voice as you can muster.
✔ Gently pin the ferret down until he gets bored.
✔ Shake him (gently) by the scruff (reminiscent of mother ferret's practices).
✔ When all else fails, confine him to his cage and ignore him.

Ferrets enjoy being stroked in the direction the hair lies. They prefer hard stroking rather than gentle patting. Never poke fingers at their noses.

If your ferret plays too roughly, a sound thump on the nose with your forefinger, accompanied by a sharp "No," will soon advise your ferret that this is not acceptable behavior.

Bitter Apple can be sprayed onto your hands before a play session to discourage your ferret from nipping. Another method is to pick the ferret up by the scruff of the neck and use a sharp "No" if the kit nips too hard.

My tip: Never strike the ferret's body. This could cause serious injury.

BRINGING YOUR FERRET HOME

Before you bring your ferret home, you should learn as much as possible about ferrets. You should have your pet's bowls, food, and cage ready, and you should have some treats and Bitter Apple on hand.

Once you have determined where to buy your ferret, it is time to play with all the kits and adults available. Choose the one whose personality and color best suits you. Sometimes a kit seems to choose you. We once had a young couple visit our farm who very definitely wanted a silver female. However, a sable male kit flung himself into their hands every time they reached for their silver baby. They soon caved in to such delightful determination and home went the sable.

The trip home is generally enjoyable for the ferret, as ferrets love to travel. You should bring a small cardboard box with papers in the bottom and some holes punched in the sides. Add some crumpled newspapers or paper towels for the ferret to crawl under should he or she want to hide. As long as the animal seems calm, holding it part of the way home is fine. Should

Be VERY careful introducing small plastic toys to your ferret—small pieces of rubber or plastic can get chewed off and cause an obstructed bowel in your ferret. And NEVER let your ferret play with soft rubber toys.

the ferret get squirmy, place him or her into the box—the ferret may need to visit the bathroom.

Getting to Know Your Ferret

Now that you have your ferret home, it is time to get acquainted. If you have chosen a kit, remember even though he or she is used to people, the kit is still a baby. The commotion of slamming doors and ringing phones and the sensation of being alone may all be new experiences. For the first 14 weeks or so of life, a baby ferret will need its dry food moistened with water. The ferret does *not* need to go directly to a large party or every neighbor's house to be shown off. Give him or her a few weeks to get to know your family first. After that time, take your ferret anywhere anytime. An adult ferret will not need food soaked with water and may require somewhat less attention. However, remember, an adult must also get used to you, your family, and new surroundings.

When a kit wakes from a nap, allow the ferret time to go to the bathroom and eat before a play or handling session. Speak in a soothing way and pick up your ferret. Give him or her a drop of Ferretone and walk around carrying the kit on your arm. A kit—and even an adult—will enjoy seeing the new sights with you. Stroke and tickle the ferret just as you would a puppy. Carry your kit frequently, and this will pay off when the animal becomes an adult.

Allow the ferret to put its teeth gently onto you in play. Mock combat is normal. The absolute rule is if it hurts, the ferret is wrong and should be disciplined. Just like a new puppy, a young ferret must learn how rough is rough enough.

If you are going to allow your ferret free run, choose a small room and confine it there. Of course, make sure that you have ferret proofed the room *before* placing your pet into it. Refer to page 59 for a list of hidden home dangers this room should not contain. The ferret will need considerable time at first to explore the new surroundings before becoming interested in playing. Once the ferret is thoroughly familiar with this area, it will be ready to interact with you. The ferret will not need such a long exploration time after being in this area several times.

Basic Rules for Handling Ferrets

✔ Always speak in a soft, friendly manner to the ferret before picking him or her up—you do look *big* to your ferret.

✔ If the ferret is sleeping, allow the animal time to take care of litter trips and eating first.

✔ Give your ferret a treat—not every time it is picked up—but often enough that the ferret never knows when you will do something wonderful for it.

✔ Do not be afraid to roughhouse with your ferret. It is small, but ferrets are used to playing roll and tumble games together; your ferret does not want to be treated as though he or she were fragile.

✔ Do *not* put your pet down when it wants down. *You* must train the ferret. Ferrets are smart enough to train you if you allow them. If it puts its teeth onto you as a reminder (much like a cat gesture), give it a sharp "No!" If this is not sufficient, add a thump on the nose to the second "No!" or a scruff with a "No."

Playing with Your Ferret

Ferrets enjoy a variety of games. Hopping, jumping, and mock combat are normal for them. Ferrets also enjoy a good game of tug-of-war. Sometimes they will entice you to chase them and then they can chase you. Digging and burrowing—a pile of fall leaves is perfect—can elicit a hopping dance of joy on the part of your ferret. Any tube or container the ferret can crawl into and out of is fine. Hide-and-seek games seem to be a favorite.

Ouch! Baby Plays Too Roughly

Ferrets have very tough skins. Both baby and adult ferrets play quite roughly with each other, but this is the cause of most problems that occur in ferret/human play. Because the ferret has learned the level of pressure he or she may exert on brothers and sisters without making them angry, the ferret logically expects you to enjoy the same vigorous games. If you are consistent in your discipline and correct your ferret each time he or she is too rough, your ferret will soon learn to play more carefully with you. If you correct the ferret only sometimes and not others, the ferret will have a hard time understanding what you expect.

Ordinary nail clippers and cat claw scissors will both do a good job trimming your ferret's nails.

Because even a baby ferret can nip too hard, never leave a kit unsupervised with young children. Make sure the child is old enough to handle the ferret properly—including ferret training and discipline. No animal should be near the face of a young child. No animal should be near the face of a stranger at any time. Any animal can become frightened and hurt somebody. A bite to the face would be especially painful. This is true for cats, dogs, and all other pets in the home, including ferrets.

Nipping Toes

Toe nipping is the most common misbehavior of young ferrets. It seems to happen for two reasons: not making the connection between the wiggling creatures and their two-legged friend, and a desire to play chase and have interaction.

Either reason requires the same response: *firm discipline.* A sharp "No!" spoken about 6 inches (15 cm) from the ferret's face while making eye contact is most effective. If you have a toe nipper, spray Bitter Apple onto your socks and then tempt the ferret. He or she quickly learns that the enticing, wiggling creatures inside the sock taste *terrible* and loses all desire to grab them.

My tip: The real danger is that you might make the mistake of inadvertently encouraging your ferret to form the toe-biting habit. If you are amused by the first gentle nibbles and allow the behavior to continue, you reinforce a pattern that inevitably will become intolerable for you.

Toe biting must never be allowed to start as a cute game. Stop it before it gets to be a habit.

Grooming and Bathing

In recent years, ferrets have become so popular that many professional groomers and pet salons are accustomed to doing them. However, ferrets are relatively easy to groom, and you may wish to groom your ferret yourself. If so, follow these simple guidelines.

Ears and Nails

The hardest part of grooming a ferret is the care of the ears and the nails. When you clean the ears, it is best if the ferret is held by a helper. The helper should use one hand to grasp the ferret around the shoulders, forelegs, and chest in a firm, but gentle, manner. The helper should hold a bottle of Ferretone in his or her other hand and use the Ferretone to distract the ferret while the ear-cleaning procedure goes on. The scruff grip is also very effective for this task.

The tiny ears of a ferret are cleaned with cotton tips and an ear-cleaning solution suitable for ferrets or kittens. Dip the tip of the cotton tip into the solution and squeeze off any excess liquid. Then carefully place the cotton tip into the outer ear area and gently wipe

A well-groomed ferret is much more pleasant to have around than the alternative.

However, you can also use a regular nail clipper used for humans, but remember to turn the clipper sideways so it will not twist the toe when you trim the nails. Should you accidentally cut the nail too short and cause slight bleeding, apply pressure to the injured area or use a styptic pencil to stop the bleeding.

After doing the ears and the nails, you have completed the hardest grooming tasks and are ready to comb out any loose hairs on your ferret. Use a soft nylon brush to comb out the loose hairs. Brushing also stimulates the skin of the ferret.

out any debris and excess wax. Be careful not to insert the cotton tip into the ear canal as this can damage your ferret.

Cutting the nails is another important grooming task. The nails of a ferret should be cut just short of the vein. Look at a ferret's nails and you will see the red vein running down inside the nail. A cat-type nail cutter is the proper size nail clipper to use on your ferret.

Bathing

Now, you are ready to bathe your ferret. A double sink works best. Fill both sinks with lukewarm water. Wet and shampoo the ferret

Peek-a-boo! Long, narrow tubes are a favorite hideout for ferrets.

This Black-eyed White seems content just hanging around.

in one sink using tearless ferret or cat shampoo. Then rinse the ferret. Use the second sink for final rinsing to be sure that all shampoo is removed.

After the bathing is finished, you may want to use a ferret or feline flea product or a ferret cream rinse. Check your local pet store for ferret shampoos and flea products. Do not use dog products on your ferret. They are often too strong and could be dangerous. When finished, rub the ferret vigorously with a bath towel to help it dry and then keep it in a warm, draft-free room until the animal is completely dry.

Coat Changes

Ferrets change coats completely twice a year. In the young, the kit coat gives way to the first adult coat. This is a short, lightweight coat. The second coat is a long, dense, beautiful winter coat. At the time that a ferret changes into a winter coat, it puts on quite a bit of weight. After the winter months, it will reduce its food consumption, drop weight, and return to its lightweight coat. In the house, brushing the ferret often during the period when it is losing its winter coat is often tidier. Most of what would be shed out around the house will brush out easily and can be discarded.

If Your Ferret Escapes

We frequently get calls saying, "My ferret is lost. What should I do?" Beyond the obvious, "Look around the house carefully, it may just be asleep in some hidden corner," you can do some other things.

Make a list of ten places in the home the ferret cannot possibly be. Then look there. This list worked for one of our callers who found a cold and hungry pet caught in the freezer side of her side-by-side refrigerator.

Organize a search of the yard and surrounding houses. Concentrate on holes, foundations, old buildings, wood piles, and any other places that may lure your lost pet.

With a ferret in the house, always check seat cushions before sitting down.

Alert neighbors that your pet is gone.

Put up notices at stores, laundry centers, and other public places.

Alert your mail carrier and other delivery people.

Offer a reward.

At this time, you certainly will be happy that your ferret has a collar and bell so it will not be mistaken for a wild animal and killed out of fear!

Common Accidents

Several types of accidents that commonly cause injuries to ferrets occur both indoors and outdoors. Below is a list of common ones and basic first aid.

Indoors

Burns: Apply ice to the affected area and take your pet to the veterinarian if serious burns occur. For minor burns, vitamin E cream seems to be effective in promoting skin healing.

Crushing: This accident comes from being stepped on or caught in doors, springs, chair cushions, and so on. The main risk here is internal injury. Your veterinarian should examine the pet if any doubt exists.

Back injury: This also occurs from being stepped on or from accidental falls. Watch closely for signs of slow or painful movement, paralysis, or dragging a leg. Take the ferret to your veterinarian at once for this kind of injury.

Poison: In the event of accidental poisoning, speed is of the essence. Get medical help at once. Take the container of poison with you so you can be sure what chemical your ferret ingested.

The National Animal Poison Control Center at 1-900-680-0000 or 1-800-548-2423 can be a help in an emergency. You will be charged for this service.

Swallowing small objects: Foam or latex rubber objects such as pieces of athletic shoes, rubber bands, stereo speakers, headphones, pipe insulation, and doll shoes can all cause an intestinal blockage in your ferret. Vomiting is the main sign that the ferret may have an intestinal blockage. A blockage is life threatening and requires an immediate trip to the veterinarian.

Outdoors

Caught in car door: This type of accident usually results in internal injuries because of the weight and speed of the door. Always consult your veterinarian.

Don't leave your ferret alone outside—ferrets are fearless and will approach other animals that may harm them.

Fights with other animals: Usually ferrets can defend themselves quite well. They seem to know no fear. They will fight almost anything if the opponent starts it. General first aid should be used for minor injuries. For serious cuts, tears, and broken limbs, consult your veterinarian immediately.

Accidental escapes: After being lost for several days, ferrets are usually dehydrated and malnourished. Medical attention is usually needed. A checkup at this time is money well spent.

Ferrets and Other Animals

Ferret play with other animals (cross-species interaction) is one of the most intriguing aspects of ferret behavior. We have heard stories from all across the country about ferret play with cats, dogs, and other animals. For safety's sake, ferrets should generally not be left alone with small rodents or birds. However, care must be taken in the first few meetings between ferrets and their new friends.

Some dos and do nots include:

✔ **Do** restrain each animal until it is aware of the other animal or animals. Surprises can lead to tragedy.

✔ **Do** be prepared to separate the animals at the first sign of trouble.

✔ **Do not** rush the friendship. Cats especially like to approach new relationships over a long time period.

✔ **Do not** neglect other pets or make them jealous. This leads to aggressive behavior.

✔ **Do not** leave mixed groups together unsupervised until you are certain no problems will occur.

✔ **Do not** worry about mixing ferrets together except unneutered males. *All others usually get along fine.* They will play very roughly and will establish who is boss but almost never injure each other. Caution: unneutered males should never be left together, as their fighting can be life-threatening.

✔ **Do not** mix dogs who have been trained to hunt small animals with ferrets. Some of these dogs adapt well to ferrets but others are quick to kill.

Taking Your Ferret in the Car

All the ferret owners we know love to take their pets visiting. Ferrets love car trips, and we have never seen a carsick ferret.

Before taking your ferret on a trip, check your car carefully to see that it contains no ferret doors. Check the firewall under the dash, under the seats, and behind the rear seat for holes leading out of the car. Many people let their ferret have the run of the car. However, for driving and ferret safety, placing your ferret into a travel carrier equipped with a litter pan is best. Never have your pet loose in the car while opening and closing doors as the ferret could be injured or escape.

Never leave a ferret, or any animal for that matter, in the car in the summer with the windows closed. Ferrets are quite sensitive to the heat. Imagine yourself there while wearing a fur coat. If the ferret is traveling in a carrier or cage, do not let it sit in the sun for any length of time. Including in the carrier a plastic soda bottle with ice wrapped in newspaper can help keep your ferret cool in the carrier. By following these simple rules, you will love traveling with your pet as much as we do with ours.

This beautiful Silver-mitt would be difficult to part with for a long vacation!

Taking Your Ferret on Vacation

Because ferrets love to travel and are so confident and curious, they are very little trouble on vacation. You must take a portable cage with you for your convenience and your pet's safety. Use this cage to contain the ferret at the motels or homes where you are staying. Checking each location for hidden dangers is not possible, so supervise play time carefully.

A supply of dry ferret food and clean water must be offered frequently. Because water bottles leak and cups or bowls spill, offer these at each stop.

For airline travel, an underseat cat carrier is available. This will enable you to carry on your pet. Be sure you declare your pet when making flight reservations, as airlines sometimes limit the number of pets allowed on the plane.

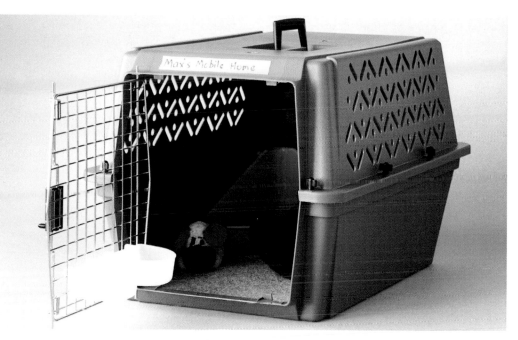

Almost all motels will allow caged ferrets if you speak with them ahead of time. Advance notification will prevent maids and service people from becoming frightened if they do not know what a ferret looks like.

Traveling to Foreign Countries

The basic rules for international travel are simple. First, check with the embassy of the country you are going to visit for their rules concerning ferrets. You should also check with the United States Department of Agriculture for restrictions concerning traveling with a ferret. You will need proof of vaccination and a health certificate from your veterinarian. Also, be sure to register your pet with U.S. Customs before leaving.

A comfortable travel cage is the first thing you'll need if you're considering bringing your ferret on a trip.

Laws are always subject to change. Check the rules each trip before putting your pet at risk.

Do not forget to bring water and ferret food from home for the trip. Providing these will decrease your pet's stress.

Leaving Your Ferret

For One Day

In almost all homes, a one- or two-day absence—without a live-in sitter—causes no problems. Be sure to leave an ample supply of food and water in the ferret's cage. Make absolutely sure the ferret cannot accidentally spill the food and water. Have a trusted, knowledgeable friend check in at least daily to be sure all is well with your ferret friends. Research has shown the ferret to have a three-hour digestive system. This means that what the ferret eats is through its system and gone in three hours. Therefore, the ferret needs a constant supply of food or he or she becomes *very* hungry in a short period of time. Turn on a radio or television to provide some company. For a two-day or longer absence, you may need a ferret-loving person to clean the litter pan as well.

If your ferret normally has the run of the house, accustom him or her to the cage while you are home. Changing its whole routine at the same time the ferret must be alone is not fair.

For a Short Vacation

In circumstances where your ferret cannot travel with you on vacation, you should leave the animal with a good ferret sitter. The sitter should have the following information and supplies:

✔ A schedule of your ferret's normal activity times.

✔ Plenty of food.

✔ Complete instructions for how to operate cages, bowls, feeders, water bottles, and other equipment.

✔ A phone number where you can be reached.

✔ The name and phone number of your veterinarian in case of injury or illness.

✔ The names and numbers of any other ferret owners who may be able to help in an emergency.

An owner of a ferret is the first choice for a sitter, but anyone who is responsible about animal welfare can do the job. Leaving the ferret with the sitter on a trial basis for a day or so before leaving on a trip is best. This practice run will point out any problems and give you time to work out solutions before the actual trip.

For Longer Periods

For extended periods away from home, the ferret sitter must have a more thorough knowledge of ferrets. Changes in weight, diet, bowel habits, and signs of illness must be understood by the sitter.

As a general rule, you can leave your pet in a kennel familiar with cats if you cannot locate a kennel familiar with ferrets in your area. Ferret care is closer to cat care than to dog care. Of course, the care varies with the personnel, knowledge, and facilities of each kennel. The attitude of the personnel is very important. We would never leave our animals at a kennel where the staff was afraid or leery of ferrets. When we have to decide between the facilities and the staff's knowledge, we prefer a staff with a real liking for ferrets. When friends or family care for your pet, have a back-up sitter in case an emergency develops at the first home.

Neutering Your Ferret

Neutering is part of good care for your ferret. It is necessary to save the health—and life—of a female and to reduce the odor and aggressiveness of a male. The majority of ferrets sold today have already been neutered and de-scented. If you are unable to obtain a ferret that has already been altered, you will need to make arrangements with your veterinarian to have this done as soon as possible.

Female

All female ferrets must be spayed sooner or later to protect their lives. Aplastic anemia and septicemia—two diseases that directly result from prolonged heat in females—are the leading causes of death in female ferrets.

Approximately two weeks after the beginning of the heat season, high levels of estrogen cause the vulva to swell greatly. The vulva becomes enormous. If left unspayed, the vulva will stay swollen and become damp and open. This leads to the life-threatening health risks for your female. The moist enlarged opening is a natural channel for infection—which frequently leads to septicemia and death. At the same time, the prolonged high estrogen level leads to aplastic anemia.

The only way to stop the prolonged heat—and the nearly always fatal diseases associated with it—is to breed an unspayed female or repeatedly use hormones to induce ovulation. However, repeated use of hormones to cause the ferret to ovulate is dangerous to your ferret's health. Breeding a female every time she comes into heat is a great drain on her body. It too leads to severe health problems.

For these reasons, females must absolutely be spayed at some point in their lives. Spaying can be done at any age. Most veterinarians prefer that it be done before six months of age but certainly before she comes into heat. Estrus causes an increase in blood supply and enlargement of the ovaries and reproductive tract that makes surgery more risky. If your ferret should come into heat before she is spayed, your veterinarian *cannot* wait to spay the ferret until she naturally cycles out of estrus. This may take months. In the meantime, your ferret could easily die of aplastic anemia—even on the first heat.

Male

Castration of male ferrets is a simple, almost risk-free operation. It can be performed at any age, but between six and eight weeks is the ideal time. Older males require 30 days or more for the benefits of neutering to fully appear. The only reason we can see *not* to neuter males is to keep them for breeding purposes. Neutering causes a dramatic decrease in odor. A breeder male secretes large amounts of musk oil and has a noticeable odor. The fur actually appears greasy from this musk oil. Unneutered males must be bathed daily to make them acceptable as house pets.

Neutering lowers aggression. During breeding season, an intact male may injure or kill other ferrets. Both males and females may be included as victims. While no aggression is directed toward people, the male is less playful and has his mind on breeding.

Neutered ferrets are no more likely to become sluggish, lazy, and fat than unaltered animals. Ferrets gain weight at the same time they grow their heavy winter coats. They lose weight and become thinner and more active when they grow their lighter summer fur coats. These natural changes can happen at any time of the year when ferrets are kept indoors year-round.

The two most common ferrets (Sable and Red-eyed White) playing with toys and grooming, respectively.

One common trait that all ferrets share is undying curiosity.

A Red-eyed White descending from his cage.

You must train your ferret, both for the ferret's happiness and long life as well as for your own full enjoyment of your pet. For reasons of safety and hygiene, your ferret must be trained to the cage and litter box. To increase your enjoyment and the ferret's, you may also train your ferret to the leash, to the shoulder or hood, and to sit up.

To the Cage

Ferrets, unlike cats, do not mind small places. When given a choice, ferrets will curl up in a small ball in a quiet, hidden cubbyhole. This lack of fear makes them very comfortable in a cage. They need and want to be out of the cage for fun, play, and exploring, but—come nap time—they are content to return to the cage and to a dark place to curl up and rest happily.

Ferrets are much safer in a cage than loose in an empty house. The best job of ferret proofing the house still leaves open the possibility of danger from unexpected guests who may unintentionally injure your pet by stepping on a throw rug that has become a ferret cover.

To the Litter Box

Ferrets are latrine-type animals and prefer to relieve themselves in the same place every time. This instinct makes them easy to housebreak.

Housebreaking in an open area should start in a small room (a half bath is ideal). Place the litter box with some feces in it into a corner. The ferret will use it easily. Expand the space available to the ferret gradually and he or she will return to the box.

In a large house, two litter pans may be necessary. With such short legs, the ferret will appreciate not having to go too far to the box and will have few accidents.

In a cage containing a litter box, be sure the litter box entrance is flat with sides at least 3 inches (7.5 cm) high. Use a ferret litter box rather than a cat litter box. Ferret litter boxes are designed with the special needs of a ferret in mind. Place some feces in one corner, and the ferret will soon use it as a bathroom.

Ferret liter pans come in many attractive colors and can be added to your ferret's cage. If the ferret moves the litter pan around while playing, you should attach it to one corner of the cage.

Most ferrets relieve themselves within several minutes of awakening. This habit allows you to ensure that the proper facility is used. One friend of ours rewarded her ferret so often for good hygiene habits that the ferret

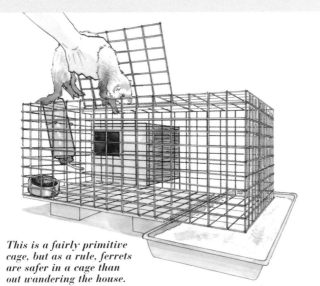

This is a fairly primitive cage, but as a rule, ferrets are safer in a cage than out wandering the house.

learned to pretend to go and would then run over for Ferretone rewards.

Should your ferret choose the wrong place in which to relieve himself or herself, use a sharp "No!" and a loud clap of the hands. Quickly place the ferret into the proper area and insist he or she stay there until he or she attends to business. Reward your ferret with Ferretone or other treats for being good.

To the Shoulder or Hood

Training to the shoulder or the hood of a jacket is the easiest way to carry your ferret on visits to new places. Attach a harness to the ferret for safety, and stand or kneel over a trash can filled with crumpled newspaper. Place the kit onto your shoulder or into the hood and allow the ferret to crawl around until he or she stops paying attention to his or her balance. When the ferret starts to fall, say *"No!"* in a loud tone and allow the ferret to fall into the newspapers. The loud *"No!,"* coupled with falling and the loud rustling of the papers, induces enough fear to make the ferret more careful. Do this several times, and then stop for that session. A ferret usually needs five or six lessons to become trained. From then on, though, the ferret will stay and be careful of his or her balance.

After your ferret is completely trained, put him or her down if it becomes excited or very active while on the shoulder or hood. Your pet may have to go to the litter box.

To the Leash

We have never known of a ferret that is leash trained like a dog is. Leash training in ferrets means keeping them from constantly fighting the leash—they will not learn to heel.

Use a lightweight leash attached to your ferret's harness (no choke chains, please) and allow the ferret to drag the leash around the house to get used to it. After this period, start restraining your pet while sitting in a chair in a familiar room. Once the animal learns the futility of fighting the leash, you are ready for a trip outside.

Start in the yard, and allow the ferret to move in a circle with you as the center point. After several ten-minute sessions over a period of several days, you should start to encourage the ferret to follow in the direction you wish to travel. Much patience is needed, but your new friend will learn!

To Sit Up

The sit-up is the easiest of all tricks to teach ferrets. It can be accomplished in a few five-minute sessions.

Start by putting Ferretone or another favorite treat onto your finger and letting your ferret lick it. Gradually raise your finger higher, and your ferret will naturally follow it. As your ferret begins to sit up, praise him generously. If he (or she) reaches out to hold your finger, take it away and start over. If you repeat the command "Sit" in a gentle voice as this is done, the ferret will soon understand the connection. Be sure to reward the animal often at first. Later, you will not have to give him or her a reward every time. Any word can be used as a command, but the same word must be used all the time.

Running Around the House

Ferrets enjoy exploring in the house. Once they have investigated everything, they will be ready to play. The typical ferret will explore by traveling around the edges of the room and visiting the underside of every piece of furniture. Attempting to interest your ferret in games in a new area is futile until the animal is satisfied he or she has seen everything in the area.

FEEDING YOUR FERRET

Ferrets basically regulate their own food consumption. Food passes through the ferret's digestive tract in only three hours, so a constant supply of food and water is necessary. The diet should consist mainly of dry ferret food. Treats are fine, but shouldn't be a substitute for a good diet.

The biggest variable in most animal foods is the amount and quality of the protein and the amount of fat in the feed. Ferrets do best with a high percentage of animal protein. Unfortunately, however, most pet foods are labeled with the total percentage of protein but not with the percentage of vegetable protein or animal protein. Some protein-rich foods contain soy products and other cereals that raise the total protein percentage to an acceptable level, but much of this is vegetable protein. With food containing high-cereal protein, the ferret is forced to consume large amounts of food in order to meet its nutritional needs. On the other hand, with foods rich in animal protein, the ferret consumes less and is better nourished. Less consumption is better for the ferret and makes cleaning litter boxes easier for you. When purchasing food for your ferret, be sure to read the list of ingredients. Choose feed with animal protein listed as the first or second ingredient. This means the food contains a higher percent of animal base protein

This Red-eyed White is wondering what goodies lie below in the picnic basket.

in the feed. Animal protein is more easily digested than vegetable proteins.

Also check to be sure the fat level in your ferret food is high enough to meet the high energy demands of your ferret.

Types of Food

We recommend feed formulated specifically for ferrets. If you are unable to obtain ferret food locally at the pet store, check in a ferret magazine or on the internet for a place to order the proper food for your ferret. The results show in the health of the ferret. Your ferret will live a longer, healthier life with the proper nutrition.

Food is available in dry form. Dry food has many advantages:

✔ It stays fresh longer and does not spoil or sour as quickly as moist food.

✔ It contains little or no milk, which is not healthy for ferrets.

✔ The dry pellets help keep the ferret's teeth and gums in good condition.

✔ The storage and feeding of dry foods is easy.

The only drawback to dry food for ferrets is that no moisture is provided and you must remember to supply plenty of fresh water to aid the ferret in digesting its food.

Caution: All baby ferrets and some geriatric ferrets require the dry pellets to be moistened with water to soften them. Barely cover the pellets with water, and leave them in the refrigerator. Within a couple of hours, the feed will be soft enough for the ferret to eat easily. You can add something to enhance the flavor if necessary.

What Ferrets Drink

Water is the liquid of choice for ferrets. Cow's milk should not be given to ferrets as it generally leads to diarrhea. Goat's milk can be given to small kits to supplement mother's milk with no ill effects.

The Food and Weight Gain Cycle

The amount of food required and the weight gain of ferrets normally vary with the seasons. Under natural lighting conditions, ferrets eat a lot and gain large amounts of weight in the fall. This prepares them for the cold winter months. The extra food is stored as fat, provid-

ing insulation for the animal during the cold winter months. In the spring, as the amount of light increases, ferrets tend to lose most of their body fat. This prepares them for summer heat—even with a fur coat.

A ferret kept inside all year-round in a light-filled house and at night near a night-light takes time to adjust. The seasonal changes do not correspond to the calendar. If the ferret has no medical problem, weight losses and gains can usually be explained by the unnatural lighting conditions under which the ferret lives. A ferret should be provided with a box, tunnel, tent, or similar item where he or she can go to get away from so many hours of light. Your indoor ferret needs a dark hidey-hole to be healthy and happy.

Special Nutrition Needs

Several times in a ferret's life cycle, its nutritional needs are special. These times occur when the ferret is very young, is pregnant, and is very old.

In the Young Animal

Kits from weaning age (6 weeks) to about 14 weeks of age require special care. Water can be added to their dry ration until it is even with the top of the food. After standing for 10 to 15 minutes, the food becomes soft and more attractive to the kit. A few drops of Ferretone or a tiny amount of kitten-milk replacer added to the mixture often stimulates the kits' appetites.

Ferrets are carnivores, so try to make sure real meat is an ingredient in your ferret's dry food.

Ferrets achieve 90 percent of their adult size in the first 14 weeks, so food consumption is very high. In fact, a kit about 8 to 12 weeks old will eat as much as an adult female.

In the young kit, we restrict treats to small licks once or twice daily to be sure all the nutritional building blocks are in place for the rapid growth. We certainly do not want any kit to wait for treats and neglect the normal food.

For slow-growing kits, goat's milk added to the soft food provides additional protein in a readily available form. Milk replacers designed for kittens are also useful. Do not forget to provide plenty of clean drinking water. Water and softened ferret pellets should be available at all times. With a kit, you must touch his or her nose to the feed several times a day to be sure the baby is eating well.

For an undernourished kit who must be weaned somewhat early, small amounts of Nutri-cal or other supplements give a high dose of calories in a small quantity. The baby should also be eating softened dry food to ensure proper nutrition. Milk replacers should be mixed in as well. Encourage increased feed consumption by placing small amounts of food onto the kit's nose or into the kit's mouth every couple of hours.

In the Older Animal

When ferrets reach five to eight years of age, a few special needs must be met. Be sure to watch older animals closely for any signs of difficulty in chewing. This can indicate dental problems. You may need to start adding water to soften the dry food to make chewing easier. Also, take the animal to the veterinarian.

A high-quality ferret food is especially important for older ferrets. With advancing age, animals do not readily absorb the nutritional levels they need. Check with your veterinarian about adding a supplement to the ferret's current diet.

In the Pregnant Animal

It is imperative that the breeding animal be of good weight—if she is too fat, there can be birthing difficulties; if she is too thin, the stress of breeding and raising young can threaten her life. Try to give the highest-quality food at this time.

Be sure your pet receives a healthy diet. Many people also add a small amount of boiled liver two to three times weekly during the last weeks of pregnancy and during the kit-raising period. A small amount of milk replacer can also be used. Do not feed high amounts of supplemental meat without adding calcium. Higher levels of phosphorus than calcium can lead to severe health problems in all mammals.

Nutrition Disorders

While proving that any particular illness is due to poor nutrition is difficult, the nutritionally deprived ferret is certainly more susceptible to nearly all diseases. Poor nutrition reduces the immune system's ability to react to diseases. High-quality feed pays off with a longer and healthier life for your ferret.

Treats

Almost any food the ferret enjoys—no bones, please—can be used for treats. The important thing to remember is that they are just that—*treats*. Giving treats should not be confused

A Blaze, a Cinnamon, and a Red-eyed White—one big happy family!

Ferrets can be easily startled.

Smile for the camera!

A Sterling Silver ferret with an appropriate toy.

A Blaze with his favorite plastic ball.

Many ferrets will accept raisins for a treat.

with providing a nutritionally balanced diet. In limited quantities, treats will not harm your pet.

Almost all ferrets enjoy Ferretone—for the recommended daily dosage, read the label. Most ferrets love raisins and will steal them at any opportunity. We once had a ferret who loved red licorice and came running at the rattle of the bag. We know of another ferret who loved lima beans—soft centers only— all skins were spit out under the counter. Frequently, ferrets are not adventuresome eaters; you may have to introduce something several times before your ferret will try anything new.

Caution: Be sure not to allow your ferret to eat any treats so hard they will not dissolve and can become lodged in the throat or the intestinal tract. Peanuts have been known to cause this type of problem in ferrets. As you know by now, ferrets tend to nibble on just about anything. For this reason, it's very important to make sure there is no poisonous plantlife in your yard where the ferret will be exploring. Following is a list of common outdoor plants that are poisonous.

Common Poisonous Outdoor Plants

American Yew	(*Taxus canadensis*)
Baneberry	(*Actaea* species)
Bittersweet Nightshade	(*Solanum dulcamara*)
Black Locust	(*Robinia pseudoacacia*)
Bloodroot	(*Sanguinario* species)
Buckthorn	(*Rhamnus* species)
Buttercup	(*Ranunculus* species)
Calla Lily	(*Zantedeschia aethiopica*)
Cherry Tree	(*Prunus* species)
Christmas Candle	(*Pedilanthus tithymaloides*)
Clematis	(*Clematis* species)
Cowslip	(*Caltha* species)
Daphne	(*Daphne* species)
English Yew	(*Taxus baccata*)
Golden Chain or Laburnum	(*Laburnum anagyroides*)
Hemlock	(*Conium maculatum*)
Henbane	(*Hyoscyamus niger*)
Honey Locust	(*Gleditsia triacathos*)
Horse Chestnut	(*Aesculus* species)
Indian Turnip	(*Arisaema triphyllum*)
Iris	(*Iris* species)
Jack-in-the-Pulpit	(*Arisaema triphyllum*)
Jimsonweed	(*Datura* species)
Larkspur	(*Delphinium* species)
Locoweed	(*Astragalus mollissimus*)
Lords and Ladies	(*Arum* species)
May Apple	(*Podophyllum* species)
Mistletoe (only the berries)	(*Santalales* species)
Monkshood	(*Aconitum* species)
Morning Glory	(*Ipomoea* species)
Mountain Laurel	(*Kalmia latifolia*)
Nutmeg	(*Myristica fragrans*)
Pokeweed	(*Phytolacca amaricana*)
Rhubarb	(*Rheum rhaponticum*)
Rosary Peas	(*Abrus precatorius*)
Snowdrop	(*Galanthus nivalis*)
Snowflake	(*Leucoium vernum*)
Sweet Pea	(*Lathyrus latifolius*)
Tobacco	(*Nicotiana* species)
Water Hemlock	(*Cicuta maculata*)
Western Yew	(*Taxus breviflora*)

CHECKLIST

The Do's and Don'ts of Ferret Ownership

Now that you have a firm grasp on what it takes to properly care for a ferret, let's cover a list of basics that every ferret owner should know:

DO:

✔ Respect your pet and his right to rest, peace, and privacy.

✔ Allow him the basic needs for healthy and nourishing food, plenty of clean, fresh water, his own toys, and a comfortable place to sleep.

✔ Protect him from harm, including teasing, harassment, or abuse from people who don't appreciate the special relationship one can develop with a pet.

✔ Learn the danger signals when meeting people or other animals for the first time so you avoid misunderstanding, fright, and possible injury.

✔ Be aware of your ferret's body language and eye expressions so you can easily detect when he is not feeling well or something is wrong.

DON'T:

✔ Disturb your ferret when he is eating or sleeping.

✔ Carry a lot of food around the house—this can be very distracting and unfair to the ferret who is on a feeding schedule.

✔ Put your face next to a ferret's face suddenly—this will startle him, and especially if the ferret doesn't know you, it can result in a bite caused by fear.

✔ Have children screaming and racing around your ferret—ferrets can get along well with children but too much commotion can cause hysteria and result in nipping.

✔ Let your ferret roam outside without supervision. They love exploring, and could very easily get lost.

✔ Poke, grab, pull ears or tail, or step on paws, especially when he is eating or sleeping.

✔ Touch a strange ferret, whether loose or on a harness, without permission.

KEEPING YOUR FERRET HEALTHY

A high-quality ferret food, plenty of fresh water, a yearly trip to a veterinarian knowledgeable in ferret care, and an observant owner will keep most ferrets safe and healthy. Ferrets are so small that you do not have time to wait and observe a problem for several days. If you notice changes in your ferret's appearance or behavior, you must act quickly to try to correct the problem.

On a daily basis, the ferret owner needs to look at the ferret carefully. Make sure the eyes are clear and bright. The whiskers should be long and soft. Short, broken whiskers can indicate poor nutrition. The ferret's ears may have some earwax, since many ferrets tend to produce a fair amount of earwax. If your ferret has a dark brown or black discharge in the ears, or frequently scratches the ears, take the ferret to the veterinarian to check for ear mites. If left untreated, ear mites can damage the ferret's eardrums. Ear mites are easily treated.

Check your ferret's teeth. The teeth should be clean, and the gums should be pink. If the gums are red or tartar has built up, go to the veterinarian. A broken tooth may not be a problem unless the tooth has turned dark or the ferret acts as though eating is uncomfortable.

Being aware of certain danger signs in your pet's health is an important part of ferret ownership.

Pick your ferret up and rub your hands gently all over the ferret to detect any lumps that could indicate a tumor or abscess. The ferret's coat should be soft rather than brittle. The skin should be clean with no black dots (which could indicate fleas) and no red, irritated areas. If you find fleas, use only products safe for ferrets or cats. Dog products are too harsh and can seriously harm your ferret.

Notice if your ferret is too fat or too thin. Has the ferret's normal food consumption changed? Has the ferret stopped eating?

Check the ferret's anal area for signs of diarrhea, bleeding, or infection. Do you see any signs of discharge from the vulva in females or from the opening of the penile sheath in males? A discharge is usually a sign of infection and calls for a visit to the veterinarian. Check your pet's stools daily. If the ferret stops having stools, this can be a sign of an intestinal blockage and is life threatening,. Notice if the ferret has diarrhea. Ferrets can easily become dehydrated unless the owner is vigilant.

Vaccinations

Any vaccination has a small risk of producing an adverse vaccine reaction. Staying at the vet's office for 30 minutes after the vaccination to be on the safe side is a good idea.

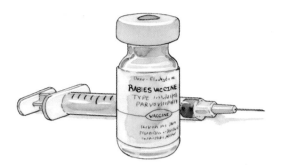

Regular veterinary checkups are of crucial importance to keep up-to-date with vaccinations.

he or she does not report the bite. If the bite is reported, most communities will kill your ferret to test for rabies even though the ferret is vaccinated. Imrab, by Rhone Merieux, Athens, GA, is an activated rabies vaccine approved for ferrets.

Reactions can include vomiting, diarrhea, and even seizures. Sometimes the ferret can develop a red spot at the actual vaccination site. If your ferret has ever had an adverse vaccine reaction, be sure to discuss this with the veterinarian before the next vaccination. The vet can give an antihistamine to reduce the potential reaction problems the next time.

Canine Distemper

You must vaccinate your ferret for canine distemper. This disease is fatal. A kit receives the first canine distemper vaccination at six to eight weeks of age and then will need shots every three to four weeks until he or she is 14 weeks of age. After that, the ferret will need a yearly booster to be protected.

Fervac-D, by United Vaccines, Madison, WI, is a USDA-approved ferret vaccine. Never use vaccines of ferret cell or low-passage canine cell origin because you could actually give your pet the disease you are trying to prevent. Never give ferrets canine combination vaccines.

Rabies

Vaccination against rabies is recommended even if your ferret never goes outside. If your ferret scratches or bites somebody and is vaccinated, this may reassure the person enough so

Diseases and Conditions

Intestinal Blockage

Intestinal blockage is one of the most common causes of death of pet ferrets. Because the ferret loves to ingest small squishy treasures and has tiny intestines, this is a frequent veterinary emergency unless the house is thoroughly ferret proofed.

If your ferret does have an intestinal blockage, he or she may produce no stool or a skinny, ribbon-like stool. Vomiting is possible. The ferret may have less of an appetite or may completely refuse food.

Dehydration is a real risk. If the ferret has eaten soft foam, the object may not show up on an X ray and cannot be palpated by the veterinarian. Exploratory surgery may be necessary. Isoflurane is the safest general anesthesia according to most ferret vets. The important issue is that you cannot wait. The ferret must get veterinary help as soon as possible to be saved.

Diarrhea

Diarrhea can be life threatening in a very short time due to the small size of the ferret. Dehydration quickly sets in. The cause of the diarrhea can be something the ferret ate,

CHECKLIST

Hidden Home Dangers

Because ferrets are so small and love dark, tight places, there are special safety considerations for them. Here is a list of problem areas.

✔ **Refrigerator motors:** Make sure your ferret cannot get under the refrigerator. They love the area close to the fan and can easily be injured.

✔ **Chair or sofa springs:** Make sure the ferret has not crawled into the springs to nap before you sit down.

✔ **Chair cushions:** Make sure the ferret is not sleeping under the cushion before you sit down.

✔ **Lumpy throw rugs:** Beware! That lump could be your dozing pet.

✔ **Buckets of Lysol and other cleaners:** Ferrets have been known to go to great trouble to drink this poison. Never leave your ferret outside his or her cage while you have cleaning supplies in use.

✔ **Small opening to the outdoors:** An adult ferret can squeeze through anything larger than 1 × 2 inches (2.5 × 5 cm). Check carefully for openings before uncaging your ferret.

✔ **Refrigerator doors:** Make sure the ferret does not decide to investigate the refrigerator or freezer while the door is open. When unnoticed, it can be accidentally shut in. Check for your ferret before closing doors.

✔ **Dryer vents** are a means of escape for many ferrets. Make sure all hoses are securely attached.

✔ **Recliner chairs** are one of the leading causes of injuries to ferrets. Never move the recliner without first locating your ferret.

---

intestinal obstruction, gastrointestinal irritation, stress, bacteria, viruses, or parasites, just to name a few possibilities. If your ferret has more than two loose stools, gather a sample and bring it and your pet to the veterinarian. A normal ferret stool is slightly soft but has form to it. The doctor will be the one to look into the actual cause and decide on the treatment. The ferret's owner is responsible for recognizing the problem and getting the ferret to the veterinarian for treatment.

Dryer vents are a common means of escape for mischievous ferrets.

Regular eye exams by your veterinarian will keep your ferret reading music beautifully.

Anytime the ferret is sick and not eating, the food should be softened with an electrolyte replacer like Pedialyte. Chicken or turkey baby food and Ferretvite or Nutrical can be added. Sometimes a tasty canned kitten food will entice the ferret to eat when added to the mix. You may even need to dab this mix onto the ferret's nose or place a tiny amount into his or her mouth to get your pet to eat. The veterinarian may need to inject some fluids under the ferret's skin to help relieve dehydration.

Epizootic Catarrhal Enteritis

Epizootic catarrhal enteritis (ECE) is a viral infection and is referred to as green slime. It affects the lining of the intestines and causes

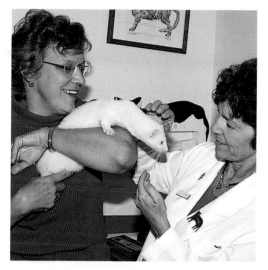

Over the years, your ferret should get to know and trust the veterinarian. After all, she is looking out for both ferret and owner!

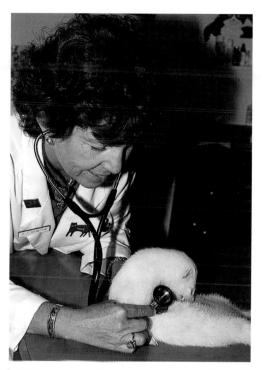

profuse mucous diarrhea. ECE is contagious and is transmitted by direct contact or by you carrying the virus on your clothes home to your ferret. Ferrets are believed to shed this virus for some amount of time after the episode has passed. The only way to keep your ferret completely safe would be to avoid contact with all other ferrets and all other ferret owners. This is not very realistic. Many people in the ferret community treat this like an inevitable childhood disease. Once the ferret has ECE, the ferret develops a long-lasting immunity against the disease.

If your ferret gets ECE, you will have to treat the diarrhea aggressively as described above or the ferret will die from dehydration. Antibiotics do not help with a virus but are often used to prevent a secondary bacterial infection.

ECE is a more serious concern for older ferrets and ferrets that have a poor immune system because of other diseases or inbreeding.

Hair Balls

Ferrets can get hair balls from grooming themselves. These can usually be prevented by giving your ferret a 1/2-inch (1.8 cm) ribbon of a cat or ferret hair ball remedy three or four times a week during shedding season. These can be found at a pet store or from your vet. Fur swallowed by the ferret cannot be coughed up in hair ball form as cats often do. If the fur is ingested, it must move on through the intestinal track or it will become lodged along the way. Prevention is the best answer because blockages can be life threatening to your pet.

Gastrointestinal Ulcers

Stomach ulcers in ferrets are often caused by a bacterium called *Helicobacter mustelae*. This is related to the bacteria linked to ulcers in humans. The ferret will need antibiotics to address this condition.

Illness occurs most often in ferrets 12 to 20 weeks of age. The stresses associated with this condition include rapid growth, diet changes, and poor-quality diets. Ferrets susceptible to this often have other diseases that make them more vulnerable. A ferret with ulcers becomes lethargic, does not eat, and becomes emaciated, dehydrated, and somewhat anemic. Black, tarry feces may stain the tail fur. If left untreated, gastrointestinal ulcers will cause your ferret to die.

Influenza

Ferrets catch the same type of colds and influenza (flu) that people catch. Like any family member, a ferret can catch the flu from you and give it back to you. The ferret usually has the good sense to drink plenty of liquid and get plenty of rest until he or she recovers. Hand washing is the best defense for everybody. Wash your hands before and after handling the ferret if anybody in the household is sick. The ferret's symptoms will be similar to yours. These include sneezing, runny nose and eyes, decreased appetite, low energy, and some diarrhea. The ferret may be ill for up to three weeks. If the ferret stops eating or if diarrhea is present, go to the veterinarian. Let your ferret rest as much as possible, give plenty of fluids, and make sure the ferret eats.

Prolapsed Rectum

Severe or chronic diarrhea and constipation can both result in a prolapsed rectum. A ferret baby fed unmoistened pellets can strain to defecate, causing the rectum to prolapse. For this reason, the feed should be moistened until the ferret is older. If the ferret's anus is protruding or irritated, have your ferret examined. Make sure the litter is not irritating the ferret. Sometimes the ferret may need a couple of stitches to keep things in place so they can heal properly.

Lymphoma/Lymphosarcoma

Lymphoma is a tumor in the lymph nodes and is the most common malignancy in ferrets. Chemotherapy has been used, but the disease is often fatal within a few months. It produces no symptoms until the disease is advanced. Your veterinarian might see enlarged lymph nodes, diarrhea, weight loss, and some general weakness. Ferrets four years old and over should have a complete blood workup annually, because this disease can be detected with a blood workup. A form of lymphosarcoma occurs in younger ferrets. Some speculation exists as to whether this is a viral or genetic issue.

Insulinoma

Insulinoma is a pancreatic tumor (or multiple tumors) that causes the ferret to secrete excessive insulin into the bloodstream. This causes the ferret to have hypoglycemia (low blood sugar). The signs are lethargy, glassy-eyed look, and hypersalivation, which causes drooling. The signs occur intermittently. Your veterinarian will be able to diagnose this condition based on symptoms and tests. Your ferret may be treated with drugs, surgery, or both. While what causes this condition is not known for sure, some experts believe some ferrets are more genetically susceptible to this condition than are other animals.

Adrenal Disease

Hyperadrenocorticoidism is adrenal gland disease. Diagnosis is based on history, signs and symptoms, imaging diagnostics, and checking the adrenal endocrine panel. A test for this is available through the University of Tennessee College of Veterinary Medicine Clinical Endocrinology Lab at the Department of Comparative Medicine in Knoxville, TN. This disease is sometimes misdiagnosed as Cushing's disease, but ferrets do not get Cushing's disease.

The symptoms to watch for include hair loss beginning at the base of the tail; hair loss that begins at the tip of the tail is often associated with other problems. The ferret can become completely bald. A spayed female's vulva may swell as if she were in estrus. The ferret is often lethargic. Your veterinarian may be able to palpate enlarged adrenal glands. Because the spleen is often enlarged in older ferrets with no medical conditions, this is not considered diagnostic for adrenal disease. Surgery is the usual treatment for adrenal disease although some other options exist if the tumor is inoperable. The cause has not been determined. Some areas being studied are the effects of diet, the possible effects of the long daylight hours inside the home, and the genetic tendencies in closely related ferrets.

Studies conducted in other countries where ferrets are not neutered show an incidence of adrenal tumors in ferrets. Therefore, early neutering does not appear to be an issue of concern.

Aplastic Anemia and Septicemia in Females

Aplastic anemia and septicemia were the leading causes of death in female ferrets before early spaying became the accepted standard. If a female is not spayed or repeatedly bred, she has about a 90 percent chance of dying in the first heat season. Because the ferret comes into estrus and does not cycle back out on her own, the prolonged exposure to high estrogen levels leads to aplastic anemia. Aplastic anemia will cause your ferret to die. To avoid this risk, purchasing a pet that is already spayed and de-scented is best. If your ferret is not already altered, contact your veterinarian immediately.

Blocked Scent Glands

If you purchase a de-scented baby, the anal scent glands were already removed. If your ferret has not been de-scented, you will need to check for the special problems that may ensue.

An unpleasant odor from your ferret that lasts only a few minutes is probably due to blocked anal scent glands. Although a ferret normally releases these glands when he or she is very frightened or during the breeding season, the animal does not normally release them at any other time. De-scenting is recommended as standard practice for ferrets.

If the ferret releases the odor from the scent glands when he or she should not, visit the veterinarian. The veterinarian will probably evacuate the glands and administer an antibiotic because an infection is probably present. If this treatment does not clear up the problem, the ferret will have to be de-scented. This means the surgical removal of the scent glands. Many people prefer to purchase a kit that is already de-scented and avoid the problem completely.

Blindness

Ferrets that are blind seem to do fairly well. If your ferret is blind, be sure to talk to the fer-

Always supervise children and pets, for the safety of both.

If your pet ferret needs surgery, be sure to follow the guidelines on page 66.

ret before picking up your pet. The most frequent cause of blindness is cataracts, which look milky white within the pupil. Blindness can be an inherited trait. If you notice a cataract, bring it to the attention of your veterinarian.

Cardiomyopathy

With cardiomyopathy, the heart muscle continues to deteriorate. The ferret needs to rest during play, and the activity level will decrease. The ferret will cough, breathe faster, and have difficulty breathing. Echocardiography is the most accurate diagnostic test. Diet and genetic factors are considered possible issues in the disease. Your veterinarian may prescribe medications that can control the progress of the disease.

Urinary Tract Infection

If your ferret drinks a lot of water or seems to be straining to urinate, he or she may have a urinary tract infection. If the urine is very dark in color, check with the veterinarian. The ferret will need to be treated or the infection can advance into a kidney infection.

Back injuries

Many accidental injuries to ferrets occur to the spine. These injuries are always serious, and the ferret should be seen by a veterinarian. Most may involve sprains, strains, or minor dislocations that respond well to extra warmth and test. Veterinarians often prescribe drugs to relax the muscles and help the pet rest. Recovery may take from two weeks to two months. More serious injuries to the back may require surgery and a prolonged recovery period. Make sure your ferret has a quiet place to rest, easy access to food and water, and does not climb and jump around, as this could cause the injury to worsen.

Surgery for Your Ferret

Ferrets tolerate surgery very well. Most problems arising from surgery are a result of delaying the decision for surgery until the ferret is weak.

Here are a few general guidelines to follow if your ferret needs surgery:

✔ If surgery is indicated, do it at once. Delay may cause the animal to become weaker and dehydrated. The problem also could become more severe as a result of delay.

✔ Do not give the ferret food or water before surgery. Follow your veterinarian's advice carefully. Your pet's life may depend on it.

✔ At the present time, no anesthetic is safer than inhalant isoflurane.

✔ Follow your veterinarian's advice for postoperative care at home.

✔ Keep the ferret warm during recovery. Loss of body temperature is a high-stress factor and can lead to setbacks in recovery and sometimes to death.

The most common surgeries performed on ferrets are:

Castration: This is the removal of the testes in males to prevent breeding and to reduce odor.

Spaying: This is the removal of the reproductive organs in females to prevent heat cycles.

Scent Gland Removal: This surgery is done to lessen odor or to remove glands that have recurrent infections.

Removal of tumors, lumps, etc.: This procedure is to remove abnormal growths that could be cancerous or that interfere with the activities of your pet. Ferrets appear most likely to acquire lymph system tumors. Chemotherapy is usually prescribed. Insulinomas, tumors of the pancreas, may be surgically removed.

Trauma repair: Surgery is indicated for the treatment of certain wounds to help them close more evenly and to promote healing.

Removal of intestinal blockages: This surgical procedure is life-saving to a ferret who has swallowed something that blocks the digestion and passing of food.

Spinal surgery: In the event of major damage to the spine, surgery can correct disk and joint problems in some cases.

Euthanasia

In the case of severe injury or debilitating illness, euthanasia becomes a painful choice. I know of no one who wants to put a loving pet to sleep, but continued suffering and pain with no hope of recovery sometimes makes this choice the right one.

Your veterinarian can use injectable drugs and certain gases to end the suffering of your pet, if necessary. Good health care, a proper diet, exercise, and care in handling can help avoid this painful choice.

REPRODUCTION AND BREEDING

Because of the aplastic anemia problems in females, the odor and aggression problems in sexually intact males, and the low odds on kit survival, the decision to breed your ferrets should not be taken lightly. Breeding should *never* be undertaken to avoid the cost of spaying or as a whim. The pet owner must first accept the risks and responsibilities involved and think, "Yes, I understand I could lose my female, but this breeding is important to me."

Although the female is not frequently lost in breeding, it *can* happen. Accepting this at the beginning is wise so that no surprises occur. You cannot change your mind halfway through the breeding.

Small- or Large-Scale Breeding?

Once you have decided that you do want to breed ferrets, you must decide on what scale. You must also decide whether you have sufficient time available to give proper care.

Large-scale breeding—colonies of 30 to 1,000 females—requires substantial time and financial investment. Quality breeding stock should be purchased with great care. Cages,

Breeding ferrets can result in beautiful, colorful critters like this one out for a walk in the grass.

buildings, water systems, and customer acquisition plans should be well thought out ahead of time.

With large-scale breeding, you will no doubt plan to sell some of your kits to pet stores. Before you even start building your cages, you should contact the U.S. Department of Agriculture, Animal, Plant, Health Inspection Service (APHIS). You must be licensed by them before you can sell even one kit to one pet store. Since they regulate your entire operation from caging to buildings to approved health plans, contacting them early to make sure your cages and buildings will meet their standards is logical.

Small-scale breeding—just a few pet ferrets— is also a serious decision. You will have to decide whether to keep your own sexually intact stud or to locate one you can send your females to. Be sure to check for any local regulations about the number of ferrets you can have in your home. In many states, you will also need a state sales tax number to collect sales tax when you sell your kits.

Check to make sure that your veterinarian will be available in case complications occur at whelping time. Your main time commitment comes when the kits are nearly ready to wean. You will want to devote the time to play with and love the babies so they are confident of people when they go to their new homes.

Unless you decide to keep all the young ferrets, you will want to place classified ads under "Pets for Sale." You must be available to answer the many questions of a new ferret owner. When people come to look at the kits, you will need to educate them concerning ferret care and handling. The seller has the responsibility of seeing that the new owners have enough information to care for their ferrets properly. If you are not prepared to devote this time to help new ferret owners learn how to care for their pets, you should not bring kits into the world. Consult your veterinarian to arrange for spaying/neutering before the kits are placed into their new homes. Spaying/neutering and de-scenting costs are generally included in the purchase price of babies sold today. Most ferret purchasers will want a written guarantee of health and neutering/de-scenting, so you will need to plan for this ahead of time.

We do not believe anyone can be successful in an animal-breeding venture if profit is the only motive. The real reason that making a profit is important is to have enough money for the animals' care and feed and to enable you to continue doing what you love to do—raising animals. Unless you are independently wealthy, profit is necessary.

If you are just breeding a few ferrets, it is not as necessary to make a profit since most people can support this from the family budget. In the author's opinion, free or very inexpensive ferrets do no service to ferrets. Since we are against the idea of people acquiring animals on a whim and perhaps regretting it later, we feel very strongly that the prospective customer must be willing to spend time to learn about the animal before purchasing one. We also feel that if customers must make a financial commitment to the animals before taking them home, they are more likely to be serious pet owners. Perhaps they will be quicker to seek veterinary care to protect their investments should this be necessary. Maybe they will be less likely to abandon an animal that they have paid good money to acquire.

Breeding One Pair

The easiest way to breed one pair of ferrets is to keep them outside year-round. They should be placed outside first in the summer so that later, as the seasons change, they can gradually become used to the cold weather. They will need a small, tight box packed with an insulating material such as straw. Check with your veterinarian about possible heartworm risks in your geographic area when housing ferrets outside. The reason ferrets are better left outside is that under natural conditions, both will most likely be in breeding season at the same time. The temperature and lights inside confuse their natural breeding cycles, and you can easily end up with one animal in breeding condition and one not. In an outside setting, your ferrets will breed in the spring and kits will be born six weeks later.

Courtship and Mating

The female ferret is ready to breed when her vulva is fully swollen and a slight moisture discharge is present. The male is ready to breed when his testicles are fully descended and have developed to their full size.

When the female is placed into the male's cage, she will seem to reject his advances even though she is in season. This is perfectly natural. The male will be very aggressive with her. He will use his teeth to grab her behind the neck. When he has a good hold, she will become limp and passive. This allows the male to mate with the female. They may continue breeding for several hours.

While the female will probably lose some hair on her neck from the biting and holding, the male should not be so aggressive as to draw blood. While an aggressive hold is necessary, tolerating a male who could injure a female is certainly not necessary.

Although one mating is usually sufficient, we recommend leaving the male and female together for up to three days.

Care During Pregnancy

After breeding, the female should be checked to make sure she has not developed any vaginal infections. If a colored discharge exudes from the vulva, take her to the veterinarian for appropriate therapy.

To be sure your female has ovulated and is starting out of estrus, check her one week to ten days after breeding to make sure the swelling of the vulva is reduced. While it may not be all the way back to normal size, the vulva should be much smaller than at breeding. If the vulva is the same size or larger, the female is not pregnant and not out of estrus. She must be rebred. Then you must check the vulva size again one week to ten days after the second mating session.

Pregnancy lasts about six weeks. For the first three to four weeks, your female will not show any particular signs of pregnancy other than the reduction of the size of the vulva. The kits grow rapidly in her body during the last two weeks. She will become round, and her stomach will feel full. She will sleep more than usual during the last week. She will be less active and may no longer want a roommate if you have a second ferret. Place her wherever she is to have the kits at least one week before delivery. She will be much calmer at whelping time if she is in familiar surroundings.

Birth and Weaning Period

When your ferret has her kits, she may or may not want you near her. However, even if she prefers to handle the birth herself, you should peek in on her to see that all is going well. *Do not* bring people she is unfamiliar with into the whelping area. You will want her to stay as quiet and calm as possible.

Some females really seem to enjoy showing off the new family. I had one ferret friend, Crystal, who would lift her little hind leg to make sure we admired all her new babies. Other females are fiercely protective of their young. If your female is snappy when she has kits, it is not because she does not love you. Right now, she is very concerned about her kits. She may be especially touchy the first few days after whelping and again after the first babies have been weaned and removed. However, she will be her usual cheerful self about one week after all the kits are weaned.

Kits are generally weaned by six weeks of age but some especially large kits can be weaned earlier. Small kits may need to wait a little longer. While the kits are still with the mother, keep a bowl of dry feed soaked with water in the cage. This way the kits become accustomed to the feed. This wet feed also keeps the mother from having to supply all the

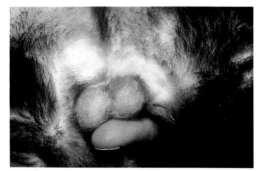

A male ferret is ready to breed when his testicles are fully descended.

A female is ready to breed when the vulva is swollen.

A mother with a litter of four-week-old kits.

Weaned kits at just over six weeks of age.

Ferrets usually have short necks, dense, soft fur, and oval-shaped heads with bright, expressive eyes.

kits' needs. The same type feed should be fed to the weaned kits.

Health Risks to the Female

The highest risk to the female occurs at whelping. If the female becomes glassy-eyed and weak at delivery time, she will need to be seen by a veterinarian. If she is unable to deliver her kits, she may have two kits that are trying to be born at the same time or she may not have strong enough contractions to expel the kits. Whatever the reason, she is in serious trouble and needs help.

Your veterinarian will probably have to perform a cesarean section (a C-section). We have never seen a female with serious delivery problems manage on her own. She will die if you do not contact a veterinarian. The C-section also carries risks for your female. The main problems with C-sections seem to be the anesthesia. An animal in a debilitated, stressed condition who weighs only 1½ pounds (0.75 kg) is not the best candidate for surgery requiring anesthesia. There are no good choices at this point. It will help if the lightest possible anesthetic dose is used.

After surgery, the ferret should be placed onto a towel or a heating pad turned to low to help her maintain her body temperature. While she will quite likely not be able to care for her kits, they can be removed from their sacs and placed onto the heating pad with the mother. The kits will not be very wiggly at first for when the mother was anesthetized, they were also. All you can do is wait and hope from this point.

Another risk to your female whether she had a C-section or vaginal delivery is mastitis. Mastitis is an infection of the milk glands. Check for mastitis by picking the female up and feeling the areas around the teats—they should be soft. Mastitis can be either acute or chronic. Acute mastitis tends to occur soon after birth or after the third week of lactation, but it can appear at any time. The milk gland becomes swollen, hard, red or even purple. This condition is painful and can become gangrenous within hours. Treatment includes surgical removal and antibiotics to save your female from death. Chronic mastitis develops slowly. The gland is firm but not painful and discolored. Little milk is available. The size of the gland now comes from scar tissue instead of from milk in the gland. The kits will generally start to become long and thin looking and will need their feed supplemented by you. Some veterinarians believe these females will never be able to nurse kits again. The kits could transmit mastitis to another ferret if they nurse. They should be bathed and separated for several hours before going to a new ferret mother if one is available.

Raising and Socializing the Young

Picking up and handling your kits often starts at three weeks of age. Even with their eyes closed, they become used to you and start to relate to you. When the kits are weaned and eating well, play with the babies. Now is the time for them to learn to expect a Ferretone treat. They will enjoy being carried and stroked.

Reread "Bringing Your Ferret Home" starting on page 33. This is your guide to socializing those kits. *Do not* simply place them into another cage and ignore them until someone takes them home. You play a large part in determining how they will feel about people in the future.

Ferret Medical History Worksheet

Ferret's Name _____

Physical Description (color) _____

Owner's Name _____

Owner's Phone # _____

Ferret's date of birth _____

Keeping a medical history on hand for each of your ferrets can help you or someone else who is taking care of your ferrets handle an emergency situation better. It's a good idea to keep this information in a safe place, along with your vaccination records.

Note: As babies, ferrets require a series of 3 Canine Distemper vaccinations and a booster shot each year after that for their own protection (Distemper is highly contagious & fatal to ferrets). Yearly rabies vaccinations are recommended. **Contact your veterinarian for more information.**

Checkup & vaccination history (note anything unusual)

Date_____Weight_____Vaccination(s)_____

Date_____Weight_____Vaccination(s)_____

Date_____Weight_____Vaccination(s)_____

Date_____Weight_____Vaccination(s)_____

Date_____Weight_____Vaccination(s)_____

Date_____Weight_____Vaccination(s)_____

Date_____Weight_____Vaccination(s)_____

Date_____Weight_____Vaccination(s)_____

Date_____Weight_____Vaccination(s)_____

Date_____Weight_____Vaccination(s)_____

Date_____Weight_____Vaccination(s)_____

Known allergies/reactions _____

_____

Surgeries performed _____

_____

Medical conditions _____

_____

Medications currently being administered & schedule _____

_____

Additional notes _____

_____

_____

EMERGENCY NUMBERS & INFO

Regular Veterinarian

Phone # of Regular Veterinarian

Name and Address of Animal Hospital

Phone # of local 24 hr veterinary facility that will see ferrets

Address of local 24 hr veterinary facility that will see ferrets

Name & Phone # of a local experienced ferret owner(s) who can answer questions

The National Animal Poison Control Center — 24 hr service by veterinarians

1-900-680-0000
($20 for the first 5 minutes, $2.95 for each additional minute)
1-800-548-2423
($30/case, credit cards only)

This form was provided by *Modern Ferret* Magazine to help ferret owners everywhere. Please make as many copies of it as you need.

UNDERSTANDING YOUR FERRET

History of Ferrets

Ferrets are members of the Mustelidae family. Other members of this diverse family are the weasel, mink, otter, sable, badger, and skunk. The scientific name of the domestic ferret is *Mustela furo.* Some disagreement exists as to who the ferrets' wild ancestors were. Scientific evidence points to two possible choices. The steppe polecat *(Mustela eversmanni)* found in Siberia and the European polecat *(Mustela putorius)* are both considered possible ancestors.

A wild cousin or relative found in the United States is the black-footed ferret whose scientific name is *Mustela nigripes.* This animal, which is on the endangered-species list, is not even considered a possible ancestor of the domestic ferret. While sable domestic ferrets have black feet, they are not closely related to the rare black-footed ferret.

The native-American black-footed ferret, *Mustela nigripes,* was listed as an endangered mammal in North America in 1967. By the mid-1970s, many feared them extinct. Because of the devotion and work of many people, the black-footed ferrets were successfully reproduced in captivity for the first time by Dr. Donald R. Kwitkowski while he was with the Wyoming Game and Fish Department at the

Ferrets are a commonly misunderstood animal, but they can make for fascinating pets.

Sybille Research Unit in Wyoming. The domestic ferrets were used to perfect some of the reproduction techniques used on the black-footed ferrets. Thank goodness this beautiful species of ferret, while still endangered, has now been successfully reproduced. Our domestic ferrets were glad to be able to lend a hand to their beautiful wild cousins.

Ferrets were first domesticated by the Egyptians in 3000 B.C. Most historians believe that the Crusaders of the tenth to twelfth centuries introduced the working ferret to Europe. These domestic ferrets may have bred with the common European polecat. The European polecat, the steppe polecat, and the domestic ferret are so closely related that they can be crossbred in the manner of dogs and wolves. Note that the offspring resulting from such crosses tend to resemble the more aggressive parent and thus do not make good pets.

Make sure your pet ferret came from a reputable source and that it was born and raised in the United States. Some foreign countries use the wild species of ferrets for fur, and these are not domestic animals. This would be the equivalent of obtaining a wolf when you thought you were acquiring a German Shepherd or a Siberian Husky.

Ferrets have been in the United States for over 300 years. They were used in the 1800s for rodent control. The *ferretmeister* would come with his ferrets to a farm or granary and release his ferrets. These working ferrets ran into the holes and hiding places of the rodents, and the rats ran out. The people would wait outside with shovels and terrier-type dogs and then kill as many rodents as they could.

Ferrets are sometimes kept on small farms and at feed mills for rodent control. The normal range of a ferret in these circumstances is about ⅛ mile (200 m) from the place it considers home. Ferrets traveling through rat tunnels leave trace odors that trigger fear in rats and mice, causing them to flee. Ferrets also face some dangers: they may become trapped in a rat tunnel. Anytime you allow your pet outside, he or she could become injured. Be sure all your ferrets' vaccinations are current, including rabies vaccinations.

Ferrets have also been used successfully to help wire planes in hard-to-reach places. Since ferrets love to enter anything that looks like a tunnel, it is a simple matter to attach a wire to the ferrets and have them run down a tunnel and return. Ferrets have been used to help run wiring in preparation for Y2K.

Ferrets have also been used in scientific research. Since they catch the same common cold and flu as humans, they have been used in medical investigations of these and other areas. Path Valley Farm has chosen not to raise any ferrets for research as we are a pets-only breeder.

Ferrets have steadily increased in popularity since the 1970s. Initially, ferrets were prized only for their abilities as ratters. As more information was made available and more people learned about ferrets, their popularity skyrocketed.

Today, some veterinarians specialize in ferrets. Certain catalogs are filled with ferret toys and products. Several excellent magazines, many informative newsletters, plus interesting internet sites are devoted to ferrets. Ferret clubs exist in nearly every area. At least two national ferret organizations promote ferret health and ferret ownership. You can attend ferret shows, which are both educational and enjoyable. Ferrets compete in conformation and color classes as well as costume classes. Fun-type classes are also held for digging, yawning, and hopping events.

*The black-footed American ferret (**Mustela nigripes**), on the right, is not an ancestor of any of the domestic ferrets discussed in this book (on left).*

Ferrets as Predatory Animals

Ferrets used to be much better predatory animals than they are today. Because they are kept primarily as pets, responsible breeders have bred only very docile adults. Many ferrets have become so gentle that we hear more and more stories of ferrets being very casual about rodents. The owners of a pet store once told me that they had a mouse escape and hide out in the ferret cage. The pet male ferret yawned and finished his nap. The unfortunate mouse then ventured into the next cage of ferrets and found a female who still had some hunting instincts left.

We know of another family who has one of the male ferrets we bred. This ferret has been completely adopted by their parakeet. The parakeet regurgitates food for him and regularly enters the ferret's cage. The parakeet pecks the ferret and initiates chase games. This ferret clearly has little hunting instinct left.

My tip: Friendships between animals that could become predators should always be supervised for the animals' safety.

Common Misconceptions

The most common misconception about ferrets is that they are European polecats bred in captivity—wild animals. As we have seen in the preceding section, this simply is not true.

Another misconception is that ferrets will establish in the wild. Ferrets have been in the United States in large numbers for over 300 years and have never been able to do this. No wild ferret colonies exist anywhere in the world. Errors probably stem from confusing the domestic ferret (Mustela furo) with the American black-footed ferret (Mustela nigripes).

Still another misconception is that ferrets who get loose will destroy thousands of rabbits. Many years ago (and even today in England), ferrets were sometimes used to hunt rabbits. Ferrets could enter rabbit holes at one end, and the frightened rabbits would exit at the other end. Ferrets never could catch many rabbits. Hunters would wait at the exit holes and get the rabbits as they ran out. Today, this practice is illegal in the United States and Canada.

External Features

Ferrets are small, furry creatures. Adult males are usually about 16 inches (40 cm) long and weigh from 3 to 5 pounds (1.5 to 2.5 kg). Females are smaller, about 14 inches (35 cm) long and about 1½ to 3 pounds (0.75 to 1.5 kg).

The ferret head is shaped like a wide wedge. Most breeders strive for a shorter-looking head by selectively breeding ferrets with the desired trait. The resulting ferrets have a wider wedge that gives the overall appearance of a shorter head. In males, the head is usually broader and less pointed than in females. The eyes are bright, clear, and expressive. Ferrets see well in dim light. They do not see well in bright light, and they cannot discriminate among colors. They can, however, be trained to discriminate among objects. According to at least one scientific report, ferrets rank near primates in object discrimination tests.

Ferrets have a total of 40 teeth. On each side are three incisors on the top and three on the bottom, two canine teeth on the top and two on the bottom, four premolar teeth on the top and three on the bottom, and one molar on the top and two on the bottom.

Let's rock and roll! Again, the very popular in-and-out routine.

This ferret looks like he could get comfortable, but this common cat litter box needs to be cut down on one side to be appropriate for a ferret.

Ferrets love to have their own small, dark place to "sack out."

Again, a cozy little nook is just what ferrets need when they are ready to relax.

The ferret neck is typically short. The body is elongated, lean, muscular, and athletic looking. The legs are short. The feet have five toes, all ending in claws. At the bottom of the feet are many tiny pads. These tiny pads may be sensitive to vibrations and help the ferret locate prey and other objects.

The body fur is dense and soft. The underlying skin is smooth. Ferrets have poorly developed sweat glands in the skin and cannot tolerate high temperatures. If you leave your ferret outside in the summer, be sure that he or she does not stay in direct sunlight and that shady spots and plenty of water are available. When in doubt, inside the house is safer for your pet.

Internal Anatomy

Ferrets are so flexible that people sometimes wonder if they have bones. Yes, they do—just like all vertebrates. Ferrets have a long vertebral column (backbone) made up of seven cervical (neck) vertebrae; 15 thoracic (chest) vertebrae; five lumbar and three sacral vertebrae in the lower-back region; and 18 caudal vertebrae in the tail. They also have 15 pairs of ribs, which you can easily feel on the front upper part of your ferret's body. They also have the other skeletal features typical of vertebrates.

The circulatory system of a ferret is unusual in one respect—only a single central artery is in the neck. Some zoologists believe that this midline vessel allows continued blood flow to the brain when the ferret turns its head a full 180°—as is its habit, especially when the ferret ventures into small tight places as it is prone to do. (Such head turning would squeeze a lateral blood vessel and lead to impaired blood flow to the brain.)

The spleen of ferrets is usually much larger than would be expected in an animal of this size. This sometimes leads veterinarians unfamiliar with ferrets to diagnose an enlarged spleen. Making this error can confuse the veterinarian's ability to make a correct diagnosis.

The part of the neck just below the skull appears to play an important part in the psychosexual system of ferrets. A mother ferret carries her kits by the skin at the back of the neck, and the kits become quiet and limp. This behavioral pattern may have developed in the ferret's ancestors as a way of lessening danger when a mother moves her kits away from predators or to a new den. Later, during adolescence, young ferrets—ages three to seven months—induce this limp and submissive state in others during mock combat, sexual play, and attempts at dominance. As adults, the male grabs the female by the back neck area to force her to submit to mating.

Intelligence and Sense Organs

Ferrets do not have very well-developed sight. They do, however, have keen senses of hearing, smell, and touch. These senses are, in fact, developed enough so that a blind ferret can cope nearly as well as a sighted ferret. A blind ferret will sniff out and explore the surroundings very thoroughly—more thoroughly than a sighted ferret. Moving furniture, cage, etc. in a blind ferret's play area is not advisable. Once familiar with the area, a blind ferret will hop, jump, run, and play much as a sighted ferret does.

Ferrets are thought to be intelligent animals, probably similar to dogs in their intelligence level. Their curiosity, play behavior, and train-ability make their intelligence readily apparent.

Because ferrets are interested in everything, they can be difficult to train. You are compet-ing with a multitude of things for their undi-vided attention.

My tip: Short training sessions are best; oth-erwise, the ferret will become bored.

Social Behavior and Play Gestures

A single ferret will amuse himself or herself with games and toys. If another pet is in the home, the ferret will make every attempt to teach it ferret games; ferrets are very social animals.

When a new ferret is introduced, ferrets will engage in hopping, jumping, clucking, and neck grabbing to establish a pecking order. The dominant ferret will drag the more submissive ferret around by the back of the neck, much as a mother carries her kits. Once this matter is settled, they can get down to the serious busi-ness of play. My mother keeps two of her fer-rets in one cage and another in a single cage. When the two are released for play time, they climb up the second cage and cluck for their other buddy to be released to play.

Ferrets like to sleep curled up together, much as you would expect to find a pile of puppies who are in the same litter. If you have four ferrets who know each other and keep them in a huge cage, all four will sleep in one crowded pile. The ferrets also need a box, sack, tube, or other structure in their cage where they can pile into a dark, safe-feeling place as part of their social behavior. An open-area hammock is great for lounging, but your ferrets need a dark place to hide out and sleep.

Mock combat and chase are the two most popular ferret games. Mock combat is very similar to the gestures of kittens. The ferret wants you to tap your hand on the ground, bouncing toward and away from the animal. The chase game is often initiated by a tug on the pants. You chase the ferret—the ferret chases you.

Tug-of-war can be initiated with a wash-cloth. Drag it along the ground, and let the ferret steal it. When you take hold again, the ferret will pull and attempt to steal it back.

A variety of photos showing ferrets at what they do best— exploring, eating, being held, and in the case of this book, mugging for the camera.

Body Language

As you get to know your ferret, you will come to associate certain stances and movements with your ferret's mood. Is your pet happy? Fearful? You can often tell by how the animal moves and acts—body language can speak volumes if you know what to look for.

Hopping, jumping, and bouncing toward you: People sometimes believe the ferret is after them. We have even heard of people who thought the caged ferret was lunging at the wires for them. Actually, the ferret is trying to entice you to play. The gesture is similar in looks to the gleeful abandon with which some kittens jump and play. The back is arched, and the ferret frequently clucks at the same time.

Running backward: This tends to happen sometimes as you go to pick up the ferret. It is either unsure of you or not too sure it wants to be picked up. When this occurs, leave your pet alone until he is ready for contact, or if a stranger is trying to meet your ferret, try giving him a small treat.

Puffing: The ferret sits on all four feet, back slightly arched, and raises all the hair until it stands straight out (see drawing opposite). Even the tail hairs stand away from the body. If two ferrets have been in a tiff, the loser does this. The ferret is trying to seem larger than he or she really is. This gesture clearly exhibits fear.

Teeth on your hand when holding: Your ferret is asking to get down or telling someone, "Be careful, big person. I am bigger than I look!" The best course of action is to tell the ferret, "No!" or "Careful," and continue holding him or her. We do not want to teach the animal that this is the way to get down.

Swings head quickly to smell hand when picked up: Ferrets do not see particularly well. When a giant picks up a ferret, the animal wants to inspect the giant more closely. Be sure to talk to your ferret before picking him or her up, and don't do anything too abruptly.

Sound Language

Ferrets make several types of noises. Like body stances and movements, you can learn to identify and understand them.

Clucking: This ranges from a soft "Cluck, cluck" to a "Dook, dook" noise. We have seen ferrets do this when they

Hopping and jumping toward you are normal ferret play gestures.

When a ferret is puffing, all of its fur stands on end.

are very happy and also when they are angry. This seems to be an all-purpose noise depending on the situation. When angry or excited, the noise seems a little higher pitched and more rapid.

Hissing: This is more of a fear noise than an aggression noise. Mother ferrets hiss when they are disciplining their kits. Soft words and comforting reassurance are the best way to deal with a hissing ferret.

Screaming: A ferret who is accidentally stepped on or terrified can scream. This sounds almost like a child who throws his or her head back and screams, "Ahhhh!" This sound is shrill

A ferret that is unsure of itself (or you) is likely to retreat a few steps.

and piercing, and is sure to get you to jump quickly off the ferret's tail, if that is the problem. Again, soft words and reassurances are definitely needed here. This is not the time to yell at the ferret.

APPENDICES

Appendix 1:
A Word About Regulations

Most states have always grouped ferrets with other pets such as dogs and cats and have never established separate regulations governing their keeping. Other states once had laws specifically regulating ferrets but have changed these laws in the light of scientific evidence. A few states, however, still do classify ferrets separately from other common domestic pets and have specific laws concerning ferrets. Such separate governmental regulations stem from misconceptions about ferrets and antiquated laws based on these misconceptions.

At one time, the idea that ferrets were wild animals that could establish in the wild was widely held. At that time, laws prohibiting or severely restricting ferrets were passed in many areas. Since then, interested people have presented the facts to state legislatures or in a court of law. In most cases, the laws have been changed.

In the past, for example, a few states expressed concern over any possible rabies problems with ferrets. However, even before a vaccine was approved specifically for ferrets, there were very few documented cases of ferrets with rabies. A rabies vaccine is now approved for ferrets, so of course, this is an obsolete objection.

Before bringing a ferret home, be sure you're familiar with local laws and regulations.

Let us take a brief look at how laws were changed in a few states, starting with Pennsylvania, the state in which we live. When we first began raising ferrets in Pennsylvania, breeders and anyone who sold even one ferret had to purchase a $50 per year license from the Pennsylvania Game Commission. Anyone wanting to purchase a pet ferret had to obtain a $10 per year license from the Game Commission before they could take possession of the ferret. No set guidelines were available concerning the circumstances under which applications for licenses would be accepted or rejected. You would have to wait anywhere from one week to several months to receive a license. If you moved with your pet ferret from another state into Pennsylvania, you might not know that ferrets were under the control of the Pennsylvania Game Commission. If you were found out, your pet could be confiscated and killed. This situation was in many ways bizarre. The Game Commission was expending considerable money and personnel to regulate ferrets— money and personnel that could have been used to address other animal concerns.

To try to change this situation, we went to a local state representative who was on the Fish and Game Commission. We presented him with all the information we had gathered showing that ferrets are domestic animals not able to establish in the wild. We then testified at legislative committee meetings. As a result, a new law was passed that removed ferrets from Game Commission regulation. Pennsylvania now treats ferrets like any other domestic animals.

We have discussed this situation in detail to make the point that antiquated laws can be changed—if concerned citizens gather the scientific data and present it to the proper authorities. A brief look at action in a few states substantiates this point.

At one time, West Virginia did not allow ferrets under any circumstances. West Virginia residents often crossed into Maryland to buy a ferret and then illegally took the animal back to their home state. When a group of concerned citizens presented the scientific facts to the West Virginia lawmakers, the restrictions were lifted. A similar situation occurred in Maine. Now both West Virginia and Maine treat ferrets just like any other domestic pet.

Alaska presents an interesting case. Alaska's laws used to permit ferrets. Then, the Alaska Game Commission, operating under false assumptions about the animals, issued regulations that, in effect, said ferrets were no longer allowed. It was not a law but an interpretation by the Game Commission that ferrets fell under wildlife rules. After a few years, the Commission confiscated the ferrets of a dedicated ferret pet owner. He presented scientific information showing that ferrets were domestic animals to the Alaska Fish and Wildlife Commission, but the regulations were not changed. Frustrated, the pet owner took the case to court. Over 400 scientific references were produced showing that ferrets are domestic animals—not wild—and the judge removed the ferrets from wildlife regulations.

However, a few states still have laws restricting ferrets. In most of these states, efforts are under way to examine the scientific literature and adjust the laws. A few cities have their own local regulations. Contacting your local pet stores to obtain the names of nearby ferret organizations is a good place to start if you live in or move to an area with ferret regulations. They can put you in touch with people working on presenting current scientific data to modify these regulations.

Because local regulations can vary and change, checking before you buy is best. Pet stores are usually aware of the status in their area. Ferret magazines and internet sites can also give you useful information about legislative efforts in your area.

Appendix 2: Litter Training Your Ferret

One of the challenges of keeping a new ferret is to train him to use the litter box and not leave you any "surprises" in corners, behind doors, or under your bed. It's not that easy a procedure, and it will take you some time, but remember, the more diligent you are with litter box training up front will pay off for many years to come.

Getting Started

Assuming you already have a cage, you'll need to put a litter box in one of the rear corners. A triangular, high-backed box seems to work well, as long as one side is low enough to allow your ferret easy access (see photo on page 17). Also, it's a good idea to secure the box to the cage so it's in no danger of being flipped.

Put an inch or so of litter in the box, and cover the rest of the cage with comfortable bedding materials—old soft rags and t-shirts work well. Hopefully, the ferret will use the litter box on his own, because if he considers the rest of the cage a place for sleeping he will not likely evacuate there. If you do notice the ferret pooping outside the box, try to reach him in time and physically move him into the box. If you don't make it in time, when you do notice place some of his waste in the litter box and leave it there. It's important to remove waste from the soft part of the cage promptly—the sooner your ferret learns it does not belong there, the better.

Life Outside the Cage

Once it's play time, let the ferret out for fifteen minutes or so, and put him back in the cage to see if he needs to do his business. If not, you'll want to put the ferret back in his cage every 30 minutes or so to see if he needs to use the litter box. If not, fine. But when he does use the litter box, be sure to praise him strongly, and give him a small treat. This will reinforce that use of the litter box is a good thing.

Once the ferret learns to use the box in the cage, add a second litter box somewhere else in the room. It's not a bad idea to put sample droppings in the new box to let him know this is another option for him when he needs to go. Again, it's a good idea to place him inside from time to time at first and praise him when he does the right thing.

If He Forgets

No ferret is perfect, and occasionally your ferret may make a mistake. If you're lucky enough to catch him "getting prepared" rather than actually "in the act," be sure to physically rush him to a litter box. If you're too late and you find a mistake outside the box, discipline him (see page 31). You might grab his scruff, say "No" or "Wrong" in an authoritative tone, and give him a time-out in his cage for five or ten minutes to get the point across.

Remember, if you work at litter training when you first get your ferret, you will be much happier in the long run!

INFORMATION

Useful Addresses
United Ferret Organization (UFO)
P.O. Box 606
Assonet, MA 02702
e-mail: Defret@aol.com
Shows, clubs, general and health information,
supplies, newsletter

Path Valley Farm, Inc.
P.O. Box 233
Willow Hill, Pennsylvania 17271
Ferret information, ferret food, supplies
www.pathvalleyfarm.com

Modern Ferret Magazine
P.O. Box 1007
Smithtown, NY 11787
www.modernferret.com

STAR*Ferrets
(Shelters That Adopt and Rescue Ferrets)
P.O. Box 1832
Springfield, VA 22121-0832
e-mail: starferret@aol.com
www:netfopets.com/starferrets.html
Send a self-addressed, stamped envelope
for a free listing of your state's ferret clubs,
shelters, veterinarians, and resources

American Ferret Association
P.O. Box 255
Crownsville, MD 21032-0233

Internet
Ferrets United Network
www.ferretnetwork.com
Information and links to ferret-related
web sites

Ferret Central
www.ferretcentral.org
Information and links to ferret-related
web sites

The Ferret Mailing List
To subscribe, send e-mail to
ferret-request@cunyvn.cuny.edu
asking to be added to the list

Usenet Groups
rec.pets
rec.pets.ferrets
alt.pets.ferrets

Ferrets will get into just about everything, so be sure to keep any valuable equipment (say, laptop computers) in a safe place.

Useful Literature

Biology & Diseases of the Ferret, James G. Fox, D.V.M. Lea & Febiger, Philadelphia, 1988. The standard work on the subject, this volume is intended primarily for veterinarians.

Ferrets, Rabbits, and Rodents Clinical Medicine and Surgery, Elizabeth V. Hillyer and Katherine E. Quesenberry. W.B. Saunders, Philadelphia, 1997.

About the Author

The author, E. Lynn "Fox" Morton, received her teaching degree in special education and is an R.N. Her love for animals led her to devote her full-time efforts to raising and breeding ferrets. She currently raises ferrets in a small mountain valley in south central Pennsylvania. She has also co-authored several articles in conjunction with the National Zoological Park, Smithsonian Institution, Washington, D.C.

Photo Credits

Joan Balzarini: 28 (middle r), 36 (top), 44 (top r), 45, 53 (bottom r), 61, 84 (bottom), 85 (top l). Norvia Behling: 2–3, 4, 8 (top l), 9 (top/bottom l), 21 (bottom r), 24, 32, 36 (bottom), 44 (top l, bottom), 48, 56, 80, 84 (top l/top r), 88. Gerry Buscis/Barbara Somerville: 8 (top r), 12, 17 (bottom), 20, 28 (top, bottom l/r), 29, 37, 41, 52 (bottom l), 81 (top), 85 (bottom), 92. Aaron Norman: 65, 73 (bottom l/r). Path Valley Farms: 8 (bottom), 16, 21 (top r), 53 (top), 64, 72, 73 (top), 84 (middle r). Modern Ferret magazine: 9 (bottom r), 40, 52 (top/bottom r), 53 (bottom l), 60, 68, 76, 81 (bottom), 85 (top r), 93. Super Pet/Pets International, Ltd.: 17 (top), 21 (left).

Cover Photos

All cover photos by Norvia Behling.

Note of Warning

This book deals with the keeping and care of ferrets as pets. In working with animals, you may occasionally sustain scratches or bites. Have such wounds treated by a doctor at once.

Ferrets, like all animals, can have external parasites, some of which can be transmitted to humans or other pets. Always check with your veterinarian if you suspect problems. When acquiring any new pet, an early medical examination is a good investment.

Ferrets must be watched very carefully during the necessary and regular exercise period in the house. To avoid life-threatening accidents, be particularly careful that your pet does not gnaw on any electric wires.

Ferrets, like all other pets, must be watched carefully when they are near infants. Caution is required at all times—both when children are sleeping and when they are awake. The only completely safe pet for a young child is a teddy bear. Never put any pet near a child's face.

Acknowledgment

I am grateful to Matthew Vriends, Gerry Buscis, and Barbara Somerville for the many suggestions that have improved this book. I especially thank the many wonderful ferret owners who have worked so hard to make the world safer for their furry friends! Let us all continue to strive for a safe, healthy and happy world for the critters who own us.

"10 Tips for New Ferret Owners" on pages 10–11 and the "Ferret Medical History Worksheet" on page 75 ©Modern Ferret magazine (www.modernferret.com). Used with permission.

All inquiries should be addressed to.
Barron's Educational Series, Inc.
250 Wireless Boulevard
Hauppauge, NY 11788
http://www.barronseduc.com

International Standard Book No. 0-7641-1050-0

Library of Congress Catalog Card No. 00-025042

Library of Congress Cataloging-in-Publication Data
Morton, E. Lynn.
    Ferrets : everything about purchase, care, nutrition, diseases, behavior, and breeding / E. Lynn ("Fox") and Chuck Morton ; illustrations by Michele Earle-Bridges.—Rev. / by E. Lynn ("Fox") Morton.
       p. cm.
    ISBN 0-7641-1050-0
    1. Ferrets as pets. I. Morton, Chuck. II. Title.
SF459.F47 M67   2000
636.9'76628—dc21   00-025042

Printed in Hong Kong
9 8 7 6 5 4